Meaning in culture

International Library of Anthropology

Editor: Adam Kuper, University College London

Arbor Scientiae
Arbor Vitae

A catalogue of other Social Science books published by Routledge & Kegan Paul will be found at the end of this volume.

Meaning in culture

F. Allan Hanson
Associate Professor of Anthropology,
University of Kansas

Routledge & Kegan Paul
London and Boston

First published in 1975
by Routledge & Kegan Paul Ltd
Broadway House, 68–74 Carter Lane,
London EC4V 5EL and
9 Park Street,
Boston, Mass. 02108, USA
Set in Monotype Times
and printed in Great Britain by
Butler & Tanner Ltd, Frome and London

ISBN 0 7100 8132 4

and this is for
Katie, George, and Brian

Contents

Preface

One important view of social science — represented by thinkers like Dilthey, Collingwood and Weber, among others — holds that the critical thing about human phenomena is that they are intrinsically meaningful. This is taken as grounds for distinguishing human affairs sharply from natural phenomena, for the latter are deemed to lack inherent meaning. This book attempts to work out the *logic* of a social science which purports to explore the intrinsic meaning of human phenomena; more specifically, it is concerned with a particular form of such a social science, which will appear before too many pages are past under the label 'institutional analysis.' My argument will be sympathetic to institutional analysis because, properly laid out, I think it is a legitimate and important way to study human phenomena. In addition, it is the way which happens to appeal to me most.

A claim that human phenomena have intrinsic meaning — which meaning should be a major object of our investigation — immediately confronts a series of questions which are ultimately philosophical in nature. The chapters which follow are attempts to frame those questions clearly and to resolve them. One such question asks where this meaning is located. Is it entirely with the agents, so that a human event can have neither more nor less meaning than is attributed to it by its perpetrator(s)? Or is there also some meaning in culture of which natives are unaware? And if so, does that imply that culture is some kind of superorganic entity with ends of its own? These issues are discussed in Chapter 1.

Then there is the question of cultural relativism. If human phenomena are intrinsically meaningful, presumably to be fully understood that meaning should be grasped internally, in its own terms, rather than according to alien criteria. But can we possibly grasp the intrinsic meaning of events in cultures radically different from our own? How can we evaluate the morality of deeds or the correctness of concepts in their own terms, if that involves standards of ethics and of truth different from ours? How can we even *understand* what is said and done in an alien culture if we do not share its criteria of rationality and intelligibility? These convoluted questions growing from cultural relativism form the subject of Chapters 2 and 3.

Finally, if human phenomena have intrinsic meaning while natural phenomena do not, can the study of such meaning be scientific? One school, call it idealist, holds that precisely because the focus of the human studies is on intrinsic meaning, the methods of science are not applicable to them. Another school, the positivist, holds that scientific procedures are appropriate — indeed, necessary — for the objective study of *all* phenomena, human as well as natural. In some variants, positivism even banishes the study of meaning in human affairs as unscientific. Disenchanted with the polar extremes, scholars such as Max Weber have attempted to chart a synthesis of idealism and positivism, wherein the intrinsic meaning of human phenomena remains the prime object of study in an investigation which nevertheless qualifies as scientific. These issues form the subject of Chapter 4.

By the end of Chapter 4, my aim is to have established institutional analysis as a mode of inquiry which focuses on the intrinsic meaning of human phenomena, which enables us to go well beyond native awareness in quest of such meaning (but not at the expense of reifying culture into a purposive being), which entails understanding of alien cultures in their own terms (in the only coherent sense that phrase can have), and which is thoroughly scientific.

In format, this can almost be seen as two books in one. Each of the first four chapters is divided into the main text and a section called 'further remarks.' In every case, the major thread of my argument is developed, without digression, in the main text of the chapter. Other issues, important but somewhat tangential to the mainstream of discussion, have been placed in the further remarks. In this way, readers who want only the prime argument of the book can have it by confining themselves to the main text of each chapter. Those readers with more than passing interest in the philosophy of social science can get a wider and deeper view of what is being said by reading also the sections of further remarks.

One terminological remark. The word 'native' is used fairly frequently in this book. Occasionally that word has a pejorative connotation, not unlike that of 'primitive.' No such connotation is meant here. By 'native' I mean nothing more than a person who was born and raised in a given society. In the sense I use the term, every human being is a native: of Nepal, Tahiti, Uruguay, the United States, the United Kingdom, and so on.

Studies leading to this book have represented my major research interest during the past five years or more, and have been pursued at the Universities of Kansas, Pittsburgh, and Oxford. I wish to thank the Institute of Social Anthropology at Oxford for its hospitality during our stay there in 1970, and Rom Harré, Rodney Needham, Paul Heelas, and especially the late E. E. Evans-Pritchard for assistance with my studies. Particular thanks are due to Gilbert Ryle for his stimulating encouragement and comments on the first three chapters. I am grateful to the University of Pittsburgh for an Andrew Mellon Postdoctoral Fellowship in 1972–3, to the Department of Anthropology there for its warm hospitality, and to G. P. Murdock, Alexander Spoehr, John Roberts, Hugo Nutini, and Keith Brown for their comments on various chapters, discussion of key issues and other assistance. Thanks are due to the University of Kansas for speeding my studies via three research grants plus sabbatical leave in 1972–3. Members of the anthropology and philosophy departments provided valuable criticism and suggestions during lectures on Chapters 1 and 2, an extended dialogue with Michael Young sharpened my thinking on relativism, and James Woelfel kindly commented on Chapter 2. Certainly I owe more to Rex Martin than to any other scholar. Through our several joint seminars, our collaboration on the essay from which Chapter 3 is derived (Hanson and Martin, 1973), and his comments on most of the other chapters, he has been my prime partner and best critic in the philosophy of social science.

More personally, my parents and my brother Ervin supported the study in important ways and, as in all things, my wife Louise helped me most. She participated in the development of ideas with a keenly critical eye, she insisted that we take advantage of research opportunities although it meant moving our family for extended periods and running financial risks, and her steady confidence carried me through moments of uncertainty.

Chapter 1

The subject matter
of social science*

Individual and institutional questions

Philosophers and social scientists have long debated the nature of the
subject matter with which disciplines like social and cultural anthropology, sociology and history deal. Do systems of belief and of
social relations, cultures, historical eras, civilizations have special
existence in their own right, or are these concepts merely convenient
shorthand for the more tangible stuff of individuals engaging in bits
of shared and repetitive behavior? This question is often thought to
threaten the territorial integrity of many social sciences, for if the
latter possibility is the case then all social science is reducible to
psychology. Hence the question has an emotional charge, for the
prospect of remapping disciplinary boundaries is exciting to some
scholars and distressing to others. After briefly describing the two
sides I will contend that neither is right. There is another, preferable
way of talking about what the social sciences study and the division
of labor between them which does not get bogged down in perplexing
problems about the ontological status of cultural things.

* Portions of this chapter were presented at the IXth International Congress of
Anthropological and Ethnological Sciences. They will appear under the title
'Meaning in Culture' in *The Concept and Dynamics of Culture*, ed. Bernardo
Bernardi, in press. Grateful acknowledgment is made to Mouton & Co., The
Hague, for permission to print them here.

A rationale for those holding that culture has its own special existence was provided in the early nineteenth century by Auguste Comte (1864). This is the view that reality comes in levels. Each level represents an emergent order of existence with laws of its own, irreducible to lower levels. Chemical reactions and combinations, for example, cannot be explained by the laws of physics. The division of scientific labor is thought to reflect layered reality, each level of existence having an autonomous discipline to study its laws. Usually the levels are identified, from simplest to most complex, as physical, chemical, biological, psychological, and social. From this perspective cultural institutions, patterns of behavior and social interaction do indeed represent a level of reality unto themselves, and disciplines like sociology and anthropology carry the mandate to explore it.

A. L. Kroeber represented this kind of thinking in anthropology. He wrote: 'the mind and the body are but facets of the same organic material or activity; the social substance — or unsubstantial fabric, if one prefers the phrase — the existence that we call civilization, transcends them utterly for all its forever being rooted in life' (1917, p. 212). Kroeber conceived of social reality — he also termed it 'superorganic' — as following a path of evolution essentially independent from organic evolution (1917, p. 210); it seemed even to have some inscrutable but intelligent purpose of its own. Concerning the strikingly regular and repetitive pattern of changes in women's fashions he said (1919, p. 261):

> What it is that causes fashions to drive so long and with ever increasing insistence toward the consummation of their ends, we do not know; but it is clear that the forces are social, and not the fortuitous appearance of personalities gifted with this taste or that faculty. Again the principle of civilizational determinism scores as against individualistic randomness.

Many empirically-minded social scientists find views like Kroeber's excessive, if not downright mystical. They hold that concepts like 'culture' and 'social system' are only abstractions from the reality of human behavior. To say that culture is a real thing which determines individual behavior and shapes its own development is to be guilty of the fallacy of reifying an abstraction and endowing it with causal influence over the very thing from which it was originally abstracted (Bidney, 1944, pp. 41–3).

If collective concepts like culture are merely abstractions from individual behavior, then cultural phenomena ought ultimately to be explicable in psychological terms. Such is the view of Melford Spiro, who has argued that 'cultural heritage' does not refer to anything that is not already covered by the term 'super-ego' (1951, p. 36). George Homans argues that social and cultural phenomena can be explained by the propositions of behavioral psychology (1964; 1967, pp. 36–43, 60–4, 73, 103–4), while George P. Murdock analyzes them according to psychological considerations such as the satisfaction of basic needs and drives, habit formation and learning (1965, pp. 83–4, 96–101). Recently Murdock has even recommended the abandonment of concepts like culture and social system as 'illusory constructs' with no more utility and validity than notions like phlogiston (1971, p. 19).

There is no need to opt for either of the polar positions just described, for there is a better way of looking at the subject matter of social science. As David Kaplan outlined it, this perspective involves the denial of the Comtean position that reality comes in levels or layers. Instead, the division of labor among the sciences stems from variations in our point of view. One way of asking questions about human things produces answers in psychological terms, another way produces them in cultural terms (Kaplan, 1965, see also Kaplan and Manners, 1972, pp. 128–33, and Parsons and Shils, 1951, pp. 239–40).

I term this the distinction between individual and institutional questions. It can readily be made clear with an example. One day during my fieldwork on the French Polynesian island of Rapa I was helping a few men with the heavy job of turning the soil to prepare a taro garden for cultivation. The sun was hot and we were perspiring freely. I picked up a jug of cool water I had brought and asked my comrades if they wanted a drink. They said no. When I then took a drink myself, they looked concerned and one of them told me I should not do that lest I get sick.

Now we can ask the question, why did they refuse the water and caution me against drinking? The question admits of two quite distinct answers, depending on our aim in asking it. If we want to know the Rapans' motives or reasons for acting as they did, we are asking an individual question and the answer in this case would be simply that they wanted to avoid illness both for themselves and for me. On the other hand, we may want to know about the ideas which lead Rapans to believe that drinking cold water when hot and perspiring can produce illness. This is an institutional question. It is not about people at all, but about concepts in their own right. In this case the answer would detail the Rapan system of ideas relating health to body temperature, which in turn is affected by various foods. One implication of these ideas is that drinking cold water when the body is hot and perspiring can adversely affect bodily temperature and hence endanger health. To summarize the difference between individual and institutional questions: individual questions relate to the motives, intentions, reasons people have for doing what they do; institutional questions concern concepts, forms of organization, patterns of behavior seen in relation to each other.[1]

What then of the reality of culture? Well, culture exists in the same way that beliefs, values, customs, forms of social and economic organization exist, for culture is the organized total of such things. But that is beside the point, because the peculiarly social sciences do not stake their claim for existence upon having a separate chunk of reality to investigate. They study the same reality that psychology studies. The difference between them is that psychologists ask individual questions about that reality whereas sociologists and their kinsmen in anthropology and history ask institutional questions of it. In asserting this I do not wish to quibble about disciplinary boundaries, such as arguing whether psychological anthropology is a branch of anthropology or psychology. The only point I wish to make, and stress, is that sociocultural investigations are not reducible to psychological ones because the institutional questions asked in the former are different from and irreducible to the individual questions asked in the latter.

Discussions I have had with numerous people indicate that this is a point where I am likely to be misunderstood. The Comtean concept of levels of reality is pervasive and extremely difficult to dislodge; it or something like it has not uncommonly led people to think that institutional questions are on a higher or more abstract level of analysis than individual questions. That point of view, which I definitely do not hold, results in an argument something like the following. One first undertakes analysis at the individual level, accounting for the raw data of human behavior by the interests, intentions, habits, needs and drives of the persons who engage in that behavior. Then one moves 'up' to the institutional level of analysis. At this level one derives or infers the customs, concepts, forms of social organization and other institutions which compose the culture by a process of abstraction from the shared habits, drives, intentions, etc. which one posited at the individual level.

Hence institutional or cultural analyses are thought to be abstracted from individual or psychological analyses, as depicted in Figure 1. It is but a short step from here to the proposition that our statements about cultural institutions are reducible to, or explicable in terms of, individual or psychological considerations, because the former were abstracted from the latter in the first place. From this point of view, of course, my assertion above that sociocultural investigations are not reducible to psychological ones would be false.

FIGURE 1

Let me reiterate as plainly as I can: I do not accept the argument of the foregoing two paragraphs. For one thing, people's needs, drives, intentions, and their psychological characteristics (the gratification of creature comforts, the aim for standing in the eyes of one's fellows, the nature of emotional stability and the ways in which it can be disrupted) seem quite constant among all men and hence are not adequate to account for the great variety of different cultural beliefs, values, symbols, and forms of organization found around the globe. As I make the distinction, individual and institutional questions do *not* represent different levels of analysis. Institutional or cultural investigations are no further removed from the raw data of human behavior than individual or psychological investigations are. Each kind of analysis results from a particular perspective on those data. The one asks about the nature of the drives, reasons, intentions, needs that people manifest in their behavior; the other asks about the structure of the values, norms, symbols, customs, roles, relationships manifested in that same behavior. While they both involve abstraction from the data, the two perspectives are not arranged one above the other but side by side, on the same 'level,' as Figure 2 shows.

Note especially that from this point of view, and quite unlike that expressed by the first diagram, institutional analyses are not abstracted from individual analyses and hence are not reducible to them. One does not 'pass through' individual questions on the way to asking institutional ones. This is the critical feature which distinguishes the view I am advocating from other positions discussed here. For all their differences, both those who would reify culture

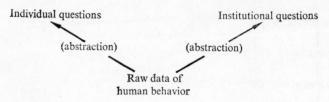

Individual questions   Institutional questions

(abstraction)   (abstraction)

Raw data of
human behavior

FIGURE 2

into a thing in itself and those who would reduce culture to psychological considerations agree that cultural statements are in some sense on a higher level than psychological statements. That view I reject categorically. Indeed, it logically must be rejected if one reasons from the view that the differences among the sciences stem from different perspectives with which we approach reality rather than from the Comtean idea that those differences reflect actual levels of empirical reality.

While there are still plenty of psychological reductionists around, today it is difficult to find a scholar who can fairly be said to reify culture. Later in his career Kroeber explicitly shifted to a view similar to that advocated here (1952, pp. 23, 112). And although Leslie White has been accused not only of reifying culture but also of deifying it (Bidney, 1950), as I read him White is driving at a distinction not so much between kinds of substance or levels of reality as between ways of inquiring into human phenomena. There is no clearer statement of the distinction between individual and institutional questions than his (L. White, 1959, p. 231, his italics; see also 1969, p. 77):

When things and events dependent upon symboling are considered and interpreted in terms of their relationship to human organisms, i.e., in a somatic context, they may properly be called *human behavior*, and the science, *psychology*. When things and events dependent upon symboling are considered and interpreted in an extrasomatic context, i.e., in terms of their relationships to one another rather than to human organisms, we may call them *culture*, and the science, *culturology*.

Meaning

Thus far we have talked a good deal about questions but very little about answers. Now I want to discuss the kind of knowledge we can expect to get when we inquire into human phenomena. Of special interest will be whether we get the same kind of answers when we ask individual and institutional questions.

It has frequently been argued that there is a fundamental difference between human and natural phenomena. As Collingwood character-ized it, natural events have only an 'outside,' whereas human events have also an 'inside' consisting of the thoughts, motives, purposes of the agents (1946, pp. 113–14). The 'inside' of human events is their intrinsic meaning. Natural events lack this meaning: the moon does not mean to orbit the earth, nor plants to grow, nor glands to secrete, they just do. But meaning is so crucial in human events that they are often unintelligible unless their meaning is known. Jones crawls about peering intently at the ground, because he means to recover a contact lens he dropped. Head-on collisions sometimes occur on the shoulder of the highway, because each driver meant to avoid a crash by swerving off the road. For Max Weber, 'the specific task of sociological analysis . . . is the interpretation of action in terms of its subjective meaning' (1947, p. 94, see also p. 101 and 1949, pp. 72–82).

'Meaning' is notorious for its multiplicity of meanings. Wittgenstein termed it an 'odd job' word which is called upon for a variety of tasks (1958, pp. 43–4); Ogden and Richards (1923) wrote a whole book about what it means. As the foregoing examples make clear, however, a very common meaning of 'meaning' when used with reference to human phenomena is intentional (see Weber, 1947, p. 93). The meaning of a human act is the agent's intention, purpose, motive, or reason for doing it.

In addition to human acts, meaning of the intentional sort is intrinsic to man-made objects, because an artifact's design crystalizes its maker's purpose. Think of the intentional meaning inherent by design in shoes, parking meters, or scissors, or of the delay and debate devoted to fixing nuances of meaning in the shape of the table at the Vietnam peace negotiations in Paris. Artifacts belong to what Dilthey called 'objectifications of life' or the 'mind-affected world:' 'everything human beings have created and in which they have embodied their thoughts, feelings and intentions' (Dilthey, 1962, p. 114; see also Weber, 1947, p. 93).[2] Dilthey also perceived meaning in the human arrangement and combination of objects. 'Every square planted with trees, every room in which seats are arranged, is intelligible to us . . . because human planning, arranging and valuing — common to us all — have assigned its place to every square and every object in the room' (Dilthey, 1962, p. 120). Thus while chairs, tables and blackboards all have their meanings, a new meaning emerges from their combination to form a classroom. And think how one can turn a seminar room into a lecture room simply by rearranging the furniture.

Dilthey's 'mind-affected world' consists of more than artifacts and their configurations. 'Its realm extends from the style of life and the forms of social intercourse, to the system of purposes which society has created for itself, to custom, law, state, religion, art, science and philosophy' (Dilthey, 1962, p. 120). In other words, that intrinsically meaningful thing which Dilthey variously and expressively referred to as 'objectifications of life,' 'objective mind' and 'mind-affected world' is nothing other than 'that complex whole' that anthropologists call culture.

At this point a problem develops with the intentional concept of meaning. This notion is adequate when the focus is on human acts or artifacts, for their meaning can be found in the purposes or motives of the people who did or made them. But how can we talk of the intrinsic meaning of cultural institutions, when no one intended them?[3] We can, of course, talk about the intentional meaning of people's *use* of institutions: why they affirm them, conform to them, manipulate them, rebel against them, and so on. These are human acts and their meaning lies in the purposes, motives, reasons of the agents. But we cannot explain the meaning of cultural institutions themselves in this manner, for here there are no intending agents.

Note that in the terminology developed above, this problem occurs precisely at the shift between individual and institutional questions. Individual questions are associated with intentional meaning, in that when we ask why people do the things they do, answers in terms of the intentional meaning of their acts are appropriate. But institutional questions focus on cultural phenomena in their own terms and not on people, so answers in terms of intentions, reasons and so on are not fitted to them. How, then, can we hold with Dilthey and others that cultures and their institutions are intrinsically meaningful?

At least some of the time, Dilthey tried to get around this problem via the notion that intentional meaning is in fact valid for cultural phenomena because institutions can intend things as well as people can. So in a passage quoted above he spoke of 'the system of purposes which society has created for itself' (1962, p. 120, see also p. 129). And Tuttle (1969, p. 75) attributes to Dilthey the view that 'the true causal forces in history are found in the motive-deliberations of the systems and not in the motive-deliberative actions of any "mere" individuals who compose the system.' But this solution is scarcely acceptable since in reifying culture not just into a thing but into something that thinks it badly distorts normal use of language. Words like 'intend' and 'deliberations' relate to the conscious thought or design of thinking agents. To apply such terms to cultural institutions, which do not think and have not consciousness, is in my judgment a confusing, unfortunate and unwarranted use of those words.

Implicational meaning

An alternative solution to the problem, and the one I advocate, is to recognize that there are many different kinds of meaning, and that the meaning intrinsic to cultural institutions is not of the intentional sort. Just what kind of meaning it is will be readily apparent if we consult a few uses of that word in ordinary language.

If someone asks, 'What was the meaning of Caesar's crossing the Rubicon?' or 'What do you mean by keeping my daughter out until 3.00 a.m.?', the concept of meaning in question is clearly of the intentional sort. But consider some other questions about meaning: 'What does the theory of evolution mean?' 'What is the meaning of the mother-in-law taboo?' 'What does it mean to have good manners?' The answers one is likely to get — dealing with matters like inaccuracy in the biblical account of creation, systems of kinship, marriage and residence, and not blowing one's nose on the table-cloth — do not relate to intentions at all. Instead, they concern the *consequences* of the things in question — the way those things are linked by logical implication to other ideas, norms, customs, patterns of behavior. Clearly this sense of meaning, which we may term 'implicational', is quite different from the intentional kind. I suggest that the meaning intrinsic to cultural institutions of all sorts — scientific theories, religious creeds and practices, social organization, ethics, and so on — is of the implicational type. Every cultural thing, like the Rapan prohibition against drinking cold water when hot and perspiring, is linked by implication to other cultural things, like a general hot-cold theory of health and disease, and therein lies its meaning.

A focus on implications produces a view of culture as a logical system analogous perhaps to a geometry or a scientific theory, albeit a rough and complex one with internal contradictions and tensions as well as reinforcements. Those authors who have noticed the implicational usage of 'meaning' tend to characterize it in logical terms: 'every proposition has systematic or logical meaning, so that its full meaning consists in all the propositions which it logically implies and which are required to define its terms' (Nagel, 1934, p. 146).[4] From this it is clear that context is critical to the idea of implicational meaning. The meaning of a whole is in its parts and their organization; the meaning of a part is in its logical articulation with other parts to form a whole.[5]

Now let me summarize the main points of my argument thus far. Human phenomena are intrinsically meaningful, and they are best understood and explained by making their meaning intelligible. However, one can ask different kinds of questions about human phenomena, and the answers involve different kinds of meaning. Individual questions are about the needs, motives, desires, aims, purposes of people; their answers are in terms of intentional meaning. Institutional questions are not about people at all. They inquire into ideas, beliefs, customs, forms of social organization as such, and their answers demonstrate implicational meaning. I want to stress that institutional questions are not reducible to individual ones, nor vice-versa. They operate from different perspectives, asking different kinds of questions and receiving different kinds of answers. Hence they neither conflict nor compete. Either approach can be pursued independently of the other; together they provide a comprehensive picture of human phenomena. Having made these distinctions, from this point on our discussion will be concerned with the logic of institutional questions.

The logic of question and answer

One important methodological issue in the study of institutional questions is the manner or format in which the meaning of cultural institutions should be described and analyzed. Since implicational meaning is essentially a matter of logical relationships, I think an excellent model for our purpose can be found in R. G. Collingwood's views on logic and metaphysics.[6] These views developed out of Collingwood's reaction to the idea that the questions of Western philosophy are timeless: that ancient, medieval, and modern philosophers have merely offered different answers to the same questions. He held that the questions themselves have changed and therefore that distortion and misunderstanding can be avoided only if one examines the views of a given thinker in terms of the questions he asked. His concern with seeing propositions in the context of questions led Collingwood to formulate a 'logic of question and answer.' In this logic (1939, p. 33):

> no two propositions, I saw, can contradict one another unless they are answers to the same question. . . . The same principle applied to the idea of truth. If the meaning of a proposition is relative to the question it answers, its truth must be relative to the same thing. Meaning, agreement and contradiction, truth and falsehood, none of these belonged to propositions in their own right, propositions by themselves; they belonged only to propositions as answers to questions: each proposition answering a question strictly correlative to itself.

Moreover, a question and its answer taken as a unit has its proper place in a 'question-and-answer complex' such that each answer gives rise to the next question in an ordered chain of thought.[7] Questions of truth and meaning should not be asked of particular answers, but of the question-and-answer complex taken as a whole (Collingwood, 1939, pp. 37–9). Nor does the process stop here. The truth and meaning of question-and-answer complexes should be determined in the context of the metaphysical beliefs of the culture or historical period: what people 'believe about the world's general nature; such beliefs being the presuppositions of all their "physics," that is, their inquiries into its detail' (1939, p. 66).

The most general metaphysical beliefs are 'absolute presuppositions'; with them the questioning activity comes to an end. Rather, this is where the process of question-and-answer begins. Absolute presuppositions are not themselves answers to any questions; they are the ultimate assumptions which give rise to all questions (Collingwood, 1940, pp. 31–3). Because they follow from no other questions or suppositions, absolute presuppositions are arbitrary. Probably this is what Wittgenstein had in mind when he wrote: 'At the foundation of well-founded belief lies belief that is not founded' (quoted in Needham, 1972, p. 71).[8]

Clearly the hallmark of the logic of question-and-answer is its emphasis on context. One should understand the beliefs, concepts and theories current in a particular age or society in the context of the presuppositions assumed and the questions asked at that time and place. Hence it is not surprising that for Collingwood metaphysics is properly a historical study. Its mandate is not to speculate about the nature of reality, but to describe systems of thought which have actually existed, to determine what their absolute presuppositions were and to demonstrate how these generate the sequences of questions and answers which were pursued (Collingwood, 1940, pp. 49–57, 63). Although Collingwood's ideas refer primarily to philosophical and scientific thought, it is easy to expand them to provide a paradigm for the institutional approach to social science. The affinities between the implicational concept of meaning and the logic of question-and-answer are clear, for both emphasize that the meaning of an idea or belief lies in its context, in its relation with other ideas and beliefs. In fact, the question-and-answer sequences that radiate out from absolute presupposition are nothing other than chains of implications. If one stipulates that in addition to verbal entities like beliefs and concepts these chains include customs, rites, forms of social organization, artifact design, manufacturing techniques and so forth, then Collingwood's logic of question-and-answer becomes an ideal model for the description and analysis of cultural institutions.

One example of the kind of analysis I have in mind is Miller's (1955) study of how absolute presuppositions held by Europeans and Fox Indians as to whether or not the cosmos is ordered hierarchically have all kinds of fascinating implications for concepts of the afterlife, the form and stability of government, the nature of collective action, relations among kinsmen, and so on. Again, the Rapan practice of carefully specifying *where* everything occurred when telling a folktale or simply recounting the events of the day, their tendency to measure the value of a man by how much land he owns, and their custom of burying the placenta under the threshold of the family home are all implications of the absolute presupposition that location is a source of order and permanence in the world (F. A. Hanson, 1970a, pp. 46-8).

Cultural determinism

Nearly every author whom we have cited in connection with an institutional approach to social science — Dilthey, Kroeber, White — has somewhere reasoned to the effect that culture works out its own purposes in history, follows its own laws, determines its own development. In discussing the world of objective knowledge (arguments, theories, systems of thought considered in their own right), Karl Popper acknowledges that these things are human creations, but characterizes that fact as 'overrated.' He continues (1969, p. 272):

> But it is to be stressed that this world exists to a large extent autonomously; that it generates its own problems, . . . and that its impact on any one of us, even on the most original of creative thinkers, vastly exceeds the impact which any of us can make upon it.

It is easy to conclude from propositions like these that culture is some sort of an entity — perhaps even an intelligent entity — in itself. Although I reject any such reification of culture, I think there is a great deal of truth in the thesis of cultural determinism. In this concluding section I want to suggest that the concepts developed above enable us to talk about how culture participates in its own development without implying that it is a superorganic thing or purposive agent in itself. As with so much else in this discussion, the distinction between individual and institutional questions is crucial to my argument at this point. One important approach to social change is via individual questions, where one seeks the motives, intentions, reasons and rewards which lead people to behave in new or different ways (see Murdock, 1965, pp. 149-50). But an equally important approach is via institutional questions, where one analyzes changing institutions in themselves, in their relations to each other. My discussion here is concerned with such institutional change.

I have contended that the intrinsic meaning of culture is implicational in nature, relating to the ways in which a culture's component institutions presuppose and imply each other. These implicational relations are dynamic in nature, modifying and developing over time. This means that a culture's present state has a good deal to do with its future state, because the institutions of any particular time have implications that become manifest in the institutions of a later time. Consider for example how a science, working within a particular paradigm or theoretical framework, develops and changes as the unforeseen implications of the theory are worked out. Or consider the vast array of implications of the invention of agriculture for population size and density, sedentary settlement patterns, occupational specialization, the growth of towns and cities. This dynamic quality of institutional implications is, I suggest, what Popper and the others are driving at when they talk about cultural phenomena generating their own problems, following their own laws or determining their own development.[9]

Because such changes are logical or implicational in nature, the evolution of a culture is intelligible after the fact. That is, one can discern the seeds of one period in an earlier period. Doing this, of course, is one of the main activities of historians and other scholars interested in social change. These points also suggest the possibility of predicting the future development of a culture. There are, however, so many variables internal to the culture and in its environment that the likelihood of predicting successfully is probably about the same as that of successfully predicting the future form of a biological species — something which also develops out of its present state.

I have said that a culture is not a completely harmonious system. Change may result from conflicts, strain or disequilibrium among institutions (Collingwood, 1940, pp. 74–5). For example, conflicting views on the age of the earth and the origin of the species on the parts of Christianity and science led to an abandonment of literal biblical interpretation of these subjects by most branches of Christianity. Again, urban life and large, close-knit kin groups seem to be incompatible, so that where the former increases the latter diminishes.

Finally, changes in a culture's environment can render institutions ill-adapted and hence set the stage for their modification. In such a case the organizational principles (or 'absolute presuppositions') may remain intact while the changed institutions may be analyzed as different and better adapted implications drawn from those pre-suppositions. For example, an ordering principle among the Tiwi of North Australia is that a man's prestige and influence depend upon how many women he can gather about him. Formerly, ambitious men strove to marry many wives for this purpose. With conversion to Christianity polygyny was replaced by monogamy. But the ordering principle persisted, in new guise: today men of importance keep a covey of *consanguineal* kinswomen (sisters, daughters, etc.) about them (Hart and Pilling, 1960, pp. 107–11). Again, I have argued elsewhere that change in the social and political organization of Rapa during the nineteenth century is a case of new manifestations derived from the same underlying principles of organization (F. A. Hanson, 1970a, pp. 200–6).

Further remarks

Methodological individualism

At numerous points this chapter touches on issues relevant to an important debate in the philosophy of social science between methodological individualism and methodological holism or collectivism. In brief and oversimplified terms, this debate asks whether all social scientific inquiry can be reduced ultimately to the behavior of individuals, or whether irreducible collective concepts and entities such as culture, institutions, and society are necessary in some investigations. To my mind much of this debate gets bogged down in the fruitless ontological question of whether culture and society really exist. Hence I avoided working through the many ramifications of this debate, in order to bring out quickly and clearly the approach which I think is the proper one: the collectivist approach in social science depends not on the existence of collective entities, but on the fact that we can and often do investigate human affairs via institutional questions as well as via individual questions. Indeed, adequately to work through the ramifications of the individualism-collectivism debate would require a book-length study in itself because questions about the nature of society and the individual's relation to it have exercised virtually every important Western social thinker from Plato, Aristotle, Augustine and Aquinas on down. During the last couple of decades a new and interesting chapter has been added to the debate by philosophers of social science. A handsome summary of their contributions has been made by Jarvie (1972, appendix).

As I have said, in my opinion the important point to make on the issue of individualism *v.* collectivism is the distinction between individual and institutional questions. Some scholars fail to make this distinction, insisting instead that all social scientific inquiry reduces to individual questions, or psychology. No one is more explicit about this than George Homans. He insists that social facts, such as norms, should always be explained by individual, psychological propositions (1967, pp. 61–4). But it is apparent that Homans thinks the only thing to explain about a norm is why people conform to it (1967, p. 60). This is, of course, an important question, and an individual or psychological approach is appropriate to it. But there are other things to know about norms, such as the historical relation between current and former norms or how a norm articulates with other norms and values in a general system of behavioral expectations. There is no room in Homans's scheme for such questions even to come up. Yet people do in fact ask them. They are institutional questions, requiring responses in terms of implicational meaning. They are not explicable by psychological propositions because they do not concern why people do what they do, but focus rather on institutions in their own right.

Together with a collaborator Homans made a similar error in thinking that the only thing to explain about a system of unilateral cross-cousin marriage is the sentiments or motives which lead people to conform to its rules. Contrary to their claim (1955, p. 59), Homans's and Schneider's explanation at the individual level by no means renders Lévi-Strauss's theory unnecessary, for Lévi-Strauss (1949) was working primarily on the institutional question of what implications various forms of cross-cousin marriage have for alliances among groups and social solidarity. To attempt to collapse institutional questions into individual ones, as Homans and Schneider do in this case, leads to a stunted social science where many important issues are simply not seen.[10]

Verifiability, use, and implicational meaning

The concept of meaning is an important issue in twentieth century philosophy. In this section I will link the implicational notion of meaning used in this book to some of the ideas about meaning advanced by philosophers.

One of the tenets of the philosophical school called logical positivism is the verifiability theory of meaning. This holds that a sentence or proposition is meaningful only if one can specify how it could be verified or falsified. Hence the propositions 'I am taller than you' and 'there are railroad tracks on Mars' are in principle verifiable and hence meaningful, although one or both may be false.[11] But the propositions 'red is industrious,' 'everything in the universe is twice as big as it was last night' or 'air has a distinctive odor that we do not notice because we have been accustomed to it since birth' are simply meaningless unless or until one can specify a means of verifying them.[12] One advantage of the verifiability theory of meaning was thought to be that it would deflect philosophy away from meaningless 'metaphysical' speculation toward more substantial concerns (Carnap, 1959).

Another philosophical theory of meaning associates it with use: to know the meaning of a proposition is to be able to use it. As Ryle said (1966, pp. 256-7): 'Learning the meaning of an expression is more like learning a piece of drill than like coming across a previously unencountered object. It is learning to operate correctly with an expression.' The use theory of meaning is associated also with Wittgenstein, who picturesquely likened meaningless sentences to knobs or wheels that turn in a machine but connect to nothing else (1968, sections 43, 269-71). That is, a sentence is meaningless if it fits with no other expressions, if it has no use or application. Imagine, for example, circumstances in which one might use the expression 'Pity the plumage but forget the dying bird.'[13]

According to Ashby (1956), philosophers subscribing to the use theory of meaning consider the verifiability theory to be outmoded, and yet there is actually very little difference between the two. As early as 1938 Schlick saw that the two theories are essentially sides of the same coin. 'Stating the meaning of a sentence amounts to stating the rules according to which the sentence is to be used, and this is the same as stating the way in which it can be verified (or falsified)' (Schlick, 1949, p. 148). That is, to state a procedure of verification is to state a use for a proposition, a way in which it links to other propositions and observations. Hence, the verifiability and use theories of meaning converge. This point has also been noted by Wisdom (1963).

The concept of implicational meaning used in this book has close affinities with the use and verifiability theories. If a sentence has no implications it has no use, because to use an expression is to exercise its implications for other sentences and for action. The connection between implicational meaning and verifiability also becomes clear when one reflects that the way to verify a proposition is to deduce one or more of its implications and then to determine if these hold true.

The verifiability theory has been criticized for being too empirical, in that if verification is thought to require an empirical experience or observation, then only those propositions are meaningful which have a bearing on the empirical world (Lewis, 1949; Barnes, 1939; Wisdom, 1963).[14] The use theory and the implicational concept of meaning are not so stringent in this regard. From their perspective a proposition can have meaning if it has implications for other propositions, even if none of the propositions in the set or system touches base with empirical reality. This point is important to the social scientist, for he occasionally encounters systems of thought and belief which are not verifiable by Western empirical standards. Or else, empirical procedures of verification are entirely irrelevant to those who adhere to such systems. Examples would be magic and witchcraft, Australian aboriginal concepts of the 'Dreaming,' and certain branches of fundamentalist Christianity. It is far more conducive to the social scientist's goal of understanding such systems to seek their meaning in the logical interconnections of their component beliefs and practices, regardless of empirical referents, than to worry whether, by some criterion utterly foreign to them, they can be counted as meaningful systems.

Of course, these differences in the concept of meaning can be readily understood. Those who defend the criterion of empirical verifiability are committed to the general logical positivist program of purging idle metaphysical speculation from philosophy in favor of clear thinking about the universe and man's attempts to understand it — specifically, his scientific attempts. The social scientist, on the other hand, aims to understand the nature of the beliefs and practices followed in a particular society, regardless of whether scientifically-oriented Westerners would judge that they stem from unfounded metaphysical speculation. For this purpose, to ask whether those beliefs and practices rest on empirically verifiable propositions is not really to the point. At any rate, to my mind the interesting thing about the verifiability, use, and implicational concepts of meaning is their fundamental sameness rather than the relatively minor differences we might detect among them.

The truth and meaning of absolute presuppositions

An element of Collingwood's logic of question-and-answer which demands further discussion is his assertion that absolute presuppositions are neither true nor false (Collingwood, 1940, p. 32).

> Absolute presuppositions are not verifiable. This does not mean that we should like to verify them but are not able to; it means that the idea of verification is an idea which does not apply to them . . . . the distinction between truth and falsehood does not apply to absolute presuppositions at all.

Occasionally Collingwood linked the concept of meaning with that of truth in such a way as to imply quite clearly that the meaningful-meaningless distinction does not apply to absolute presuppositions either (Collingwood, 1939, pp. 33, 39). Collingwood devoted much less attention to meaning than to truth in this context, but I intend to give it at least equal consideration because the concept of meaning is of such importance in this book. I have argued that social science, when it asks institutional questions should investigate the intrinsic meaning of cultural phenomena. It would be awkward indeed to conclude now that the concept of meaning is not applicable to absolute presuppositions — the most basic cultural phenomena of all. Happily this conclusion is not necessary. I will argue that the concepts of truth and meaning are indeed applicable to absolute presuppositions. This, however, represents no major break with Collingwood for I will also hold that it does not refute the basic and entirely valid point which I think he was trying to make with the concept of absolute presuppositions.

We may begin with Donagan's critique of the idea that absolute presuppositions are neither true nor false. He very reasonably points out that part of presupposing something is assuming it to be true. 'The ordinary expressions "I assume p," "I presuppose p," are abridgements of "I assume p to be true," "I presuppose p to be true." Except as such abridgements they lack definite sense' (Donagan, 1962, p. 72). This is quite right, but I think it is beside Collingwood's point because the two men ask different questions about absolute presuppositions. Donagan asks, 'do those who presuppose an absolute presupposition think that it is true?' The answer to this question is clearly affirmative. But Collingwood asks, 'are absolute presuppositions true absolutely or universally?' It is a consequence of the logic of question-and-answer, as Collingwood develops it, that this is an illegitimate question. In that logic questions about the truth of a proposition can be asked only in the context of the question which that proposition is intended to answer. Absolute presuppositions, standing at the source of all question-and-answer sequences, are not themselves answers to any question. Since they lack the requisite context, Collingwood's simple deduction is that the concept of truth is not applicable to absolute presuppositions (Collingwood, 1939, pp. 38–9; 1940, p. 32). The following passage from Collingwood's autobiography (1939, p. 66) makes it clear that he raised the issue of the truth of absolute presuppositions from an external or universal standpoint rather than from the point of view of those who adhere to them.

> The question what presuppositions underlie the 'physics' or natural science of a certain people at a certain time is as purely historical a question as what kind of clothes they wear. And this is the question that metaphysicians have to answer. It is not their business to raise the further question whether, among the various beliefs on this subject that various peoples hold and have held, this one or that one is true. This question, when raised, would always be found, as it always has been found, unanswerable; and if there is anything in my 'logic of question and answer' that is not to be wondered at, for the beliefs whose history the metaphysician has to study are not answers to questions but only presuppositions of questions, and therefore the distinction between what is true and what is false does not apply to them, but only the distinction between what is presupposed and what is not presupposed.[15]

Precisely the same points can be made with reference to meaning. As with truth, meaning is relative to the question a proposition answers. Because absolute presuppositions answer no question, the concept of meaning does not apply to them.[16]

So runs Collingwood's reasoning as I understand it. I take his basic point to be that there are no such things as absolute truth or universal meaning because the concept of truth and meaning are devoid of sense except in the context of particular metaphysical systems or world views. I agree entirely with this point, but I do not think that because of it we must conclude that the concepts of truth and meaning are not applicable to absolute presuppositions. Collingwood was led to this conclusion because he conceived of truth and meaning as moving 'upward' only. For him the truth and meaning of a proposition are relative to the question it answers, that question is to be assessed in terms of what it presupposes, and so on up to absolute presuppositions. Since there is nothing 'above' absolute presuppositions, he concluded that questions of truth and meaning are not applicable to them.

But truth and meaning are not one-way concepts. They move up *and* down.[17] The meaning of an expression is found in what it implies as well as in what it presupposes. The meaning of the social Darwinist concept of 'survival of the fittest,' for example, is partly in the theory of evolution by natural selection which it presupposes, and partly in the model of human relations which it implies. This, of course, is the idea behind implicational meaning as that concept is used in this book: the meaning of a proposition, norm, custom, any cultural institution is to be found in its logical relations with other cultural institutions, both those it presupposes and those it implies. Truth also involves implications as well as presuppositions. For example, a common scientific procedure is to verify theoretical propositions by deducing their empirical implications and then testing experimentally to determine if those implications in fact occur as predicted. As long as it passes such tests a general principle is held to be true, or confirmed. (Of course, should it fail to pass later tests, the decision about its truth is altered accordingly.)[18]

My position, then, is that the concepts of meaning and truth are indeed applicable to absolute presuppositions. Like all propositions, beliefs, and other cultural institutions, their meaning and truth is to be found in their logical relations with other propositions, beliefs, institutions. The only difference is that whereas the meaning and truth of most institutions is found both in what they presuppose and what they imply, for absolute presuppositions one must look to implications alone because, being absolute, they presuppose nothing.[19] Let me stress that this position in no way detracts from my agreement with Collingwood's fundamental point that it is not legitimate to ask if absolute presuppositions are true or meaningful in an absolute, universal or eternal sense. The concepts of truth and meaning relate to the interconnection between ideas, customs, institutions, and hence can legitimately be applied only *within* systems of thought and institutions. Because Collingwood limited meaning and truth to an 'upward' relation through presuppositions he declined to apply those concepts to absolute presuppositions; because I think that meaning and truth also move 'downward' through implications, I do apply them to absolute presuppositions. Beyond my desire to extend these ideas from systems of thought to include customs, forms of social organization and cultural phenomena of all sorts, this is the only difference I can detect between us.

Relativism

A great deal has been said in this chapter about implications. Let me conclude by drawing one important implication from the foregoing argument. If I deny the notions of absolute truth and meaning, if I maintain that these concepts apply only *within* systems of ideas and institutions — and I do so maintain — then one critical implication for social science is that all cultures and historical periods must be understood from within, in their own terms. This is the position known as cultural relativism. We arrived there via my general argument that cultural institutions have intrinsic, implicational meaning. That argument grew out of authors like Dilthey, Weber and Collingwood. Because a conclusion may be more convincing if more than one chain of reasoning leads to it, I will rapidly present another argument for internal understanding of other cultures — beginning this time with Kant and proceeding via Durkheim. From Kant comes the fundamental theorem that we do not perceive the world directly, as it is in itself. Rather our knowledge of reality is conditioned by certain *a priori* elements: the categories and forms of intuition such as time and space. These do not have their source in external reality; they are characteristics of the human mind. These *a priori* forms govern all our perceptions of the world (Kant, 1912, pp. 40–2).

It fell to Durkheim to 'socialize' Kant (see Gellner, 1962, pp. 157–8). In Durkheim's hands Kant's *a priori* forms become 'collective representations' and their origin is to be found not in the mind *per se*, but in society. From society the mind draws 'the moulds which are applicable to the totality of things and which make it possible to think of them' (Durkheim, 1915, p. 492).

The implication for understanding other cultures is clear. Thought and behavior are intelligible only in terms of the *a priori* forms which condition and govern them. Those forms, as collective representations, vary from one society to another. Therefore ideas, beliefs and actions should be understood from within — in terms of the categories of the culture from which they come. This notion of cultural relativism leads, however, to a number of serious problems. These form the subject matter of the next two chapters.

Chapter 2

Judging other cultures

The argument of the preceding chapter was that cultural phenomena have meaning in their own right, and that one important task of anthropology (and sociology and history) is to lay bare that meaning. Now I want to explore what implications these propositions have for the conduct of social science.

For one thing, institutions should be understood from within. Since the implicational meaning of any cultural phenomenon is to be found in the other institutions, beliefs, customs which it presupposes and implies, clearly it must be known in terms of its cultural context. This, of course, is the doctrine of cultural relativism: any culture should be understood in its own terms, and not according to concepts and criteria imported from another culture.

The status of relativism is anything but secure in contemporary anthropology. The notion is a Pandora's box which emits such perplexing problems that many find the relativist's stance unjustified, or even impossible. The problems with relativism come in two species. The first is evaluative. All judgments or evaluations — what is good or bad, true or false, beautiful or plain, etc — are made according to criteria. These criteria may vary from one culture to another, and so therefore may the resulting judgments. As Pascal put it, 'three degrees of latitude upset all jurisprudence; a meridian decides the truth; fundamental laws change after a few years' acceptance. . . .

Truth on this side of the Pyrenees, error on that' (Pascal, 1925, p. 216). The upshot is that the beliefs, concepts or customs of one culture should not be evaluated in terms of criteria drawn from another. This, however, can lead to uncomfortable positions. For example, it undercuts our grounds for accusing the Aztecs of error and wrong-doing in literally tearing out the hearts of human sacrificial victims in order to provide the cosmos with its necessary fuel of blood (Leon-Portilla, 1966). And what goes for cultures should go for sub-cultures, so we would likewise be barred from judgments that the Mafia should not extort and murder, or that hippies should not give LSD to their children (Yablonsky, 1968, p. 196).

The other species of problems spawned by relativism is episte-mological — it concerns the nature of our knowledge of other cultures. Cultural relativism claims that beliefs and behavior should be understood from within, according to the categories and concepts of the culture to which they belong. Assume that you are a hard-headed empiricist who holds that the only propositions which can possibly count as valid knowledge are those which are supported by empirical evidence. You are asked to understand, internally, the affirmation of a devout Christian, 'I know that my Redeemer liveth!' You ask him for his empirical evidence and he replies, 'None. It's a matter of faith.' It is probably impossible for you, the strict empiricist, to understand his belief internally because part of the context of that belief is the assumption that valid knowledge can come through faith alone, and that assumption is unintelligible to you. Similar situations certainly crop up commonly when one attempts to understand beliefs, concepts and customs in cultures different from his own. This engenders doubt that the internal understanding urged by cultural relativism is possible to achieve.

So this is our position: the elucidation of the intrinsic meaning of institutions entails a relativist approach. But cultural relativism raises problems that render it unwelcome, probably even impossible. I will tackle the evaluative problems in this chapter and the episte-mological ones in the next. I hope to show that some of the problems can be solved, while others are ill-conceived and ought never to have come up. The latter procedure will involve showing that some parts of the concept of relativism are themselves ill-conceived and should be discarded or modified. Hence, these two chapters represent more of a critical re-definition of relativism than a defense of it. Whether

or not one would still wish to call the position where we will end up
'relativism,' I will hold that it is an approach which can be expected
to yield verifiable and undistorted knowledge of the intrinsic implicational meaning of any culture, be it our own or one radically
different from ours.

The argument for evaluative relativism

Melville Herskovits and Ruth Benedict are the anthropologists most
commonly associated with the thesis that other cultures should not
be judged by standards external to them. Arguing that the categories
according to which people conceive of reality and make judgments
are cultural in origin (1948, pp. 63–4), Herskovits reasoned that
'cultural relativism . . . lays stress on the dignity inherent in every
body of custom, and on the need for tolerance of conventions though
they may differ from one's own . . . [and] the validity of every set
of norms for the people whose lives are guided by them, and the
values these represent' (1948, p. 76). Benedict concluded her famous
Patterns of Culture with the assurance that cultural relativity promises
'a more realistic social faith, accepting as grounds of hope and as
new bases for tolerance the co-existing and equally valid patterns of
life which mankind has created for itself from the raw materials of
existence' (1934, p. 278). More recently, the relativist argument has
been renewed by James Downs with his contention 'that there is no
right or wrong, that it depends on the time and place' (Downs,
1971, pp. 24–5).

Usually the evaluative facet of relativism is considered in the
context of ethics, with discussion focusing on the morality of acts
like infanticide, abandoning one's aged parents to die on the ice,
genocide. Subjects like these lend a certain drama to debate, and they
are unquestionably of critical importance. But their value-charge is
overwhelming enough that it can easily obscure the logic of evaluative relativism. Hence, although we will return to morally momentous topics later, the evaluative thesis of relativism can be set out
most clearly if we begin with relatively innocuous examples. Remember that we are concerned with evaluations or judgments of all
kinds — what is beautiful, or humorous, or exciting as well as what
is true and what is good.

The Nuer of the Sudan are intensely interested in cattle. The turn
of a horn, shape and size of a hump, color and pattern of hide

markings are all topics of endless conversation and inspirations for poetry and song (Evans-Pritchard, 1940, pp. 16–50). City dwellers of Europe and America, by contrast, are fundamentally unmoved by cattle. Now consider the question: are cattle *really* interesting? But that question itself is puzzling. Something is wrong with it. One wants to retort, 'to whom?' Things are not interesting or boring in themselves, but only in the opinions of people. Again, pre-European Polynesians valued obesity as a mark of beauty. Ranking girls (on some islands boys as well) were kept idle and fed profusely in dark huts, to produce beauties with rolls of fat unhardened by exercise and skin untanned by the sun (Danielsson, 1956, pp. 70–3). Quite to the contrary, our notions of feminine beauty favor the slender, lithe, and non-pallid. Again the general question: is obesity *really* beautiful in women? And again, there is something wrong with the question. Things are not beautiful or ugly intrinsically, but only in the eyes of people. So before the question about the beauty of fat women can be answered, we need to know whose ideas of beauty we are talking about.

These examples bring out fairly clearly the logic underpinning evaluative relativism. The judgments men make are made according to standards. Those standards may vary among cultures; therefore, so also may the judgments derived from them. Hence it is nonsensical to talk about judgments in absolute terms. They must always be considered in relation to particular sets of standards.

Now consider one more example. The Lugbara of Uganda think it is a good thing to kill strangers (Middleton, 1965, pp. 51–2). By Western morality, on the other hand, it is a bad thing to kill strangers. Again we pose the question: is it *really* good to kill strangers? This time the general question does not sound so nonsensical as in the other examples. But the relativist would argue that this is only a function of the intensity of our commitment to our own values. We are quite content to allow the Nuer their bovine fascinations and the Polynesians their penchant for plump pulchritude, but taking human lives is something else again, and we are likely to protest and to intervene regardless of Lugbara ethics. And yet, the relativist would continue, the logic here is the same as in the two other examples. Exactly as with interest and beauty, goodness does not inhere in things or events in themselves. It results from the application of *standards* — standards which are cultural in nature and which may vary from one society to another. Hence a question about the goodness of something cannot intelligibly be asked in the abstract. It has to be asked relative to somebody's ethical standards.

Let me formulate again the argument leading to the evaluative corollary of relativism — quite carefully and fully this time so that we may critically consider various positions that have been taken on it and, eventually, say something about it ourselves.

1   All evaluations or judgments that men make are made according to standards.
2   Such standards, and hence their derivative judgments, may vary in different cultures.
3   Therefore there exist no standards (of truth, beauty, goodness, humor, and so on) which are valid for all men at all times and all places.
4   Therefore we should refrain from judging the truth, beauty, goodness, humor, etc. of acts and artifacts in other cultures according to our standards.
5a We should refrain entirely from judging what happens in other cultures.
5b We should judge what happens in another culture according to the standards of that culture.

Whether one is an evaluative relativist, and to what extent, depends on how much of this argument one accepts. Propositions 1 and 2 provide only a background; one may affirm them and still not be a relativist. That label begins to apply when one goes on to affirm Proposition 3. This defines the position I call descriptive evaluative relativism (or simply descriptive relativism) in that it simply describes a state of affairs (that there exist no universally valid standards). Proposition 4 cautions against ethnocentrism and paves the way toward a pair of alternative conclusions. The less extreme, which we may call evaluative neutralism, is represented by the Proposition 5a that we should make no judgments at all about other cultures. Proposition 5b, which I call prescriptive relativism, states the stronger conclusion that we should evaluate other cultures by native standards. This latter conclusion, the most extreme form of evaluative relativism, entails that we should somehow *agree* with the Nuer that cattle are arresting, with the Polynesians that fat maidens are winsome, with the Lugbara that murdering strangers is virtuous, and so on.

With the foregoing rationale for evaluative relativism as background, I propose in the remainder of this chapter to isolate and critically examine a number of positions which have been adopted on the subject. Then I will conclude with a statement of where I stand relative to it.

Variations on universal themes

One way to cope with the question of evaluative relativism is to deny Proposition 2, which states that standards and hence the judgments flowing from them vary at different times and places. While acknowledging apparent variation, Redfield suggests that the differences among standards may only be superficial, so that standards which seem to conflict may actually be different derivations from underlying values shared by all men. As an example, one might view 'the Eskimo practice of assisting to death an aged parent as an instance of very common or universal human care for old parents' (Redfield, 1973, p. 142).[1] Redfield concludes his essay with the notion 'that the rules of conduct, in the societies the world has known so far, have their modality, their tendency toward a very general similar content' (1973, p. 143).

I would think, however, that to validate a position like Redfield's requires *specification* of the modality among rules of conduct and demonstration of how observed variations fit within the pan-human parameters. Nor is this simply a task of finding a common denominator, or net of generalization wide enough, to account for all observed conduct, because Redfield explicitly rules out some as 'inhuman,' such as Nazi cruelty and cannibalism within the in-group (1973, p. 143). But of course there then arises the difficult question of what criteria are to be employed for determining which human practices fall within the pan-human modality and which are inhuman. Moreover, evaluative relativism would by no means be laid to rest with the postulation of a few major moral principles, even if they did have universal validity, because the problem relates not just to questions of life and death, but to all judgments men make. That is, if one is to deal with evaluative relativism by claiming that cultural variations in values are ultimately derived from universal themes, one would have to specify pan-human modalities not only for what is virtuous, but also for what is true, polite, heroic, attractive, interesting, funny, erotic, and so on. While I do not claim that this is impossible, I think it is unlikely. Certainly an immense amount of research and analysis would be required to demonstrate it. In the meantime, we may pass on to other ways of dealing with the issue of evaluative relativism.

Separate but not equal

Another common way of warding off the evaluative corollary of relativism is to deny the logical connection between Propositions 2 and 3. The claim is that just because values have been observed to vary between cultures, it does not necessarily follow that the values of some cultures are no better than those of others, nor that there are no standards which are valid for all times and places. This claim is often joined with the contention that when foreign values differ from ours, ours are superior. Hence evaluative relativism is overthrown, for we are justified in judging what is done in other cultures by our more enlightened standards.

This is the position of Freeman, who finds relativism irksome and confining and holds that no true science of man is possible until we get rid of it. His own freedom from relativism is clear, for Western standards obviously inform his judgments that the amputation of little girls' fingers during New Guinea mourning rites is 'pathological' and 'barbaric' and that 'science is a system of enquiry and knowledge that transcends the separate cultures of mankind' (Freeman, 1965, pp. 65–7). While his language is more tender, Redfield operates from the same premises when he places Western civilization at the head of a humanity happily becoming more mature and humane. 'But in this sense — that on the whole the human race has come to develop a more decent and human measure of goodness — there has been a transformation of ethical judgment which makes us look at non-civilized people, not as equals but as people on a different level of human experience' (Redfield, 1953, p. 163). And from Morris Ginsberg: 'there are unmistakable differences of level as between the preliterate societies and the societies of the ancient and modern world, and as between the different societies within the modern world. The concept of levels of development involves a distinction between higher and lower' (1953, p. 133).

While these arguments may sound convincing, it is difficult to stifle suspicion when Ginsberg goes on to say (1953, p. 133): 'and it is the higher that decide that they are higher. But this, I fear, cannot be helped.' Surely we must ask, do they decide that they are higher because they really are higher, or because they are the ones that do the deciding? For example, among the values which Redfield appears to count as mature is freedom of expression and action for the individual (1953, pp. 163, 164–5). This sounds fine to those steeped in agnostic Western liberalism, but there are competing values holding that personal wishes or interests should be subordinated to more permanent and momentous ends such as the glory of God or, as Rousseau would have it, the well-being of society as a corporate whole. What grounds authorize us to place individual freedom above these other values? Again, it is a problem of standards. Until the presence of some universally valid meta-standard can be demonstrated — a meta-standard according to which our moral, aesthetic, and other values can be shown superior to the foreign standards which differ from them — any argument which claims that our standards are absolutely or ultimately better must be dismissed as lacking sense.

Logical reservations

The passage between Propositions 2 and 3 — from the fact that standards vary among cultures to the conclusion that there are no universally valid standards — has recently engaged the attention of a number of philosophers (e.g., Schmidt, 1955; Wellman, 1963; Nielsen, 1966). Whereas anthropologists like Redfield and Freeman concentrate on the content of competing or apparently competing standards, these philosophers have focused on the purely *logical* side of the matter. Nielsen, for example, argues that the information from anthropology and history regarding the ethical norms actually affirmed at various times and places does not, by itself, provide adequate evidence for a decision one way or the other as to whether standards valid for all times and all places actually exist (Nielsen, 1966, pp. 538–9). The fact that a particular act — say, killing one's invalid parents — may be judged right in some cultures and wrong in others does not logically entail the conclusion that no final decision about the virtue of the act can be made. The logical possibility remains that the judgments current in some cultures are right while those current in others are wrong. On the other hand, the simple fact that all mankind might agree about the propriety of some act, such as copulation with one's child, is not sufficient evidence for deciding the absolute morality of the act. It is conceivable that unanimous mankind may be mistaken; copulation with one's child may not be wrong after all.

Nielsen's argument is reasonable enough: even if there exist universally valid standards, it is logically possible that they might not be recognized in all cultures. Therefore the mere fact that standards vary between cultures does not necessarily entail what I have termed descriptive relativism — that there are no universally valid standards. Well then, one wants to ask, is there other evidence which can help us decide about descriptive relativism? Presumably Nielsen thinks not, for he answers the question of whether universally valid standards exist with: 'I do not know and I doubt if anyone else does either' (1971, p. 265).

Apparently Nielsen is content to leave the issue of relativism at that. But this is scarcely satisfying to the practicing social scientist who regularly encounters values and standards different from his own and who needs to think *something* about them. So while I certainly share Nielsen's ignorance about the existence of universally valid standards, I think we need to address the question of where we go from here. First of all, I do not find it terribly dispiriting that social scientific evidence does not allow an absolutely certain conclusion about the existence of universally valid standards because, after all, we have precious little entirely sure and conclusive knowledge about anything. Secondly, of the two possible conclusions that universally valid standards do or do not exist, it seems to me that the variety of standards we encounter around the world is at least more conducive to the notion that they do not. And finally, in the absence of compelling evidence for the existence of something, it is the safer intellectual procedure to assume that it does not exist rather than to assume that it does. For these reasons, I think it is prudent to accept, provisionally, the descriptive thesis of evaluative relativism — that there are no standards which are valid for all men at all times and all places — to be held as a working hypothesis until compelling evidence for their existence comes to light.

What is, is good

If we are provisionally to suppose that universally valid standards do not exist, the next question is, what are we to do about it? What implication does this have for the judgments we make? The first implication, Proposition 4 in the argument for evaluative relativism outlined above, is that we should not judge what happens in other cultures by our standards. After that come the alternative conclusions: either the neutral one that we should refrain from judging other cultures altogether (Proposition 5a), or the prescriptive one that we should make our evaluation of what happens in other cultures according to native standards (Proposition 5b). As will become clear shortly, I think the path to a tenable position on evaluative relativism is via a critical assessment of Proposition 4. For the moment, however, let me pass on to the neutralist and prescriptive theses in order to show why I think neither one of them is acceptable.

In practice it is not always clear whether particular thinkers should be classed under the neutralist or prescriptive position. In passages quoted at the beginning of this chapter, Herskovits and Benedict both speak of the equal validity of different cultures. From there one could reason to either the prescriptive or neutralist thesis, and I am not certain which route they would take. The same can be said for the fascinating 'Statement on Human Rights' prepared by the Executive Board of the American Anthropological Association,[2] which holds that cultural differences should be respected and that the moral code of one culture should not be applied to all mankind. Perhaps Sumner came closest to prescriptive relativism when he said 'everything in the mores of a time and place must be regarded as justified with respect to that time and place' (1906, p. 58) — but even this is difficult to pin down because on the same page Sumner distinguishes good mores from bad ones. At any rate, the neutralist and prescriptive theses are clearly distinguishable in principle, and I will discuss them separately.

Evaluative neutralism can be dismissed rapidly with the criticism that it is impossible to achieve. This is especially apparent when it is recalled that we are talking not just about moral matters but about evaluations of all kinds. Whether working in the field or reading a report, we simply cannot avoid finding some things interesting and others boring, some praiseworthy and others reprehensible, some attractive and others displeasing. And these judgments are inevitably made according to the analyst's own standards. Hence evaluative neutralism is not a viable option to anyone who is concerned with the actual practice of social science.

Certainly the practical criticism that it is impossible to achieve applies with as much force to prescriptive relativism as to evaluative neutralism. In this case, however, I want to pursue a more theoretical line of argument. It leads to the conclusion that prescriptive relativism is really not relativist at all, but the unwitting application of certain Western standards instead.

The ancient Aztecs practiced human sacrifice on a large scale. Asked if they were justified in this, the prescriptive relativist would claim to decide according to Aztec standards and, on that basis, he would reply 'yes.' My contention, however, is that his judgment does not really stem from the application of Aztec standards at all. First of all, notice that he and the Aztecs do not share precisely the same conclusion. If one were to ask an ancient Aztec, the reply would doubtless be 'human sacrifice is justified,' whereas the prescriptive relativist would say 'human sacrifice is justified *for the Aztecs.*' Indeed, his relativist principles necessitate that proviso, for they would certainly prevent him from holding that human sacrifice is justified for, say, the Quakers — whose standards disapprove it.

Pursuing the matter a step further, we may ask *why* human sacrifice is justified. The Aztec would reply that human sacrificial blood is the fuel without which the world would soon succumb to cataclysmic destruction. Human sacrifice is therefore justified as the necessary means of staving off the end of the world. The prescriptive relativist would answer quite differently. He would almost certainly not agree with the Aztec theory about the end of the world. Instead, he would show how Aztec beliefs, standards and values dictate human sacrifice and then argue that human sacrifice is justified (for the Aztecs) because any people is justified in doing what its beliefs, standards and values dictate.

Because the relativist arrives at his justification by a route totally different from theirs, we can scarcely say that he frames his judgment according to Aztec standards. In fact, there is immense disagreement between the two parties. The relativist does not agree with the Aztec notion about the end of the world, and very possibly the ancient Aztecs would not agree with the relativist's idea that every people is justified in doing what its standards, beliefs and values dictate. That idea is not derived from Aztec culture; it comes from the relativist's own culture and is nothing other than a standard of *tolerance* taken to rather extreme limits. Understood in this light, it is clear that prescriptive relativism actually contradicts descriptive relativism rather than being a logical consequence of it. The relativist's axiom of tolerance — that any people is justified in doing what its standards dictate — is itself a standard which he seeks to apply to all peoples at all times and all places, and which he must therefore assume is universally valid. But the descriptive thesis of relativism holds precisely that there are *no* universally valid standards, and that would apply to a standard of tolerance as much as to any other. For these reasons, I hold that the prescriptive thesis of relativism is not really relativist at all.

Understanding and disagreeing

We have now worked entirely through the argument for evaluative relativism outlined near the beginning of this chapter, and we have yet to find a satisfactory position on the issue. Now I want to suggest that the reason for our failure is that cultural relativism properly has no evaluative corollary at all. Relativism is an epistemological concept only: it concerns our *understanding* of other cultures but has no systematic implications for how we *judge* them.

Another way of making this point is to return to our formal argument for evaluative relativism, especially Proposition 4. Following the notion that universally valid standards do not exist (a notion I accepted as a working hypothesis), Proposition 4 held that therefore we should not judge what is done in other cultures by our standards. This of course is anthropology's honored caution against ethnocentrism. Yet I will contend that it is precisely here that the argument for evaluative relativism goes astray. First of all, Proposition 4 is not logically entailed by Proposition 3. The assumption that there are no universally valid standards carries no logically necessary implication at all about how the standards which do exist should be applied. Secondly, insofar as it is conducive to the notion that our judgments should be made by standards other than our own, Proposition 4 is nonsense. As I have stressed before, a judgment or evaluation can be such only with reference to standards. It can be *my* evaluation only if it is according to *my* standards — standards I accept as valid. You may evaluate according to different standards. If I know what your standards are I can understand your evaluation, can explain it to others, and so on. But as long as you affirm the standards involved and I do not, it remains your evaluation and not mine. No evaluation can sensibly be called mine if I do not accept it as valid, that is, if I do not affirm the standards involved and their application in this case.

But if Proposition 4 is to be rejected, what position should we take on evaluative relativism? A position which recognizes, as Max Weber clearly saw, that the relativist prescription to *understand* something in its own terms is not the same as, and does not entail, *agreeing* with it. ' "Understanding all" does not mean "pardoning all" nor does mere understanding of another's viewpoint as such lead, in principle, to its approval' (Weber, 1949, p. 14). Relativism directs that we understand cultural phenomena from within: Nazi genocide of the Jews according to some theory about semitic conspirators who threatened the Aryan race, cannibalism according to beliefs such as that one can acquire another's virtue and valor by eating him, acupuncture according to a theory about the desirability of equilibrium among airs or substances which flow through the body in a complex network of channels. But internal understanding by no means implies agreement with such ideas and practices.[3] We may understand them perfectly and still find them heinous, false, ridiculous, clumsy, boring, etc. These judgments we make according to *our* criteria — the only criteria we can use if they are to be our judgments.

Cultural relativism does tend to color our evaluations in one way. Although it is by no means a logically or practically necessary consequence, internal understanding usually enlarges one's tolerance for alien beliefs and customs. I insist, however, that any standard of tolerance which informs our evaluations is *our* standard; it is not indigenous to the culture under study (although that culture may also have a standard of tolerance more or less similar to ours . . . or it may not), nor is it some meta-cultural standard with universal validity. When we confront an alien belief, custom, or artifact which is deemed to be true, good, or beautiful by indigenous standards but false, bad, or ugly by ours, we should *understand* it in its own terms (as that notion is defined in the next chapter), but our *evaluation* of it must derive from our standards. If our standard of tolerance is stronger than our standard which fosters disapproval, our attitude toward the matter will be quiescent. If the latter standard is stronger — if we find the matter literally intolerable — then we are likely to voice our criticism and, depending on the degree of our disapproval and other considerations such as our power relative to theirs, we may even attempt through persuasion or force to change that thing in their culture which we find repugnant. Throughout, the standards which inform our decisions and actions are ours and there is nothing more to be said on that point. It may be comforting to clothe those standards with universal validity, so that we can certify their application to those we are trying to change even if they don't recognize them (God is on our side; we're doing this for their own good). But if such a procedure is pleasant, it is also a delusion.

Further remarks

The recent history of relativism

The doctrine of cultural relativism has had a curiously chequered career. It has provided anthropologists, sociologists and historians with a multitude of insights into other societies and other eras and it is an effective antidote to intolerance born of narrow-mindedness. Small wonder that the vast majority of anthropologists number relativism among the essential ingredients in the anthropological point of view.[4] And yet, cultural relativism has received at least as many recriminations as recommendations. The moral philosopher Eliseo Vivas indicts relativism as 'intellectually and morally irresponsible,' 'an incoherent philosophy,' and 'not only false but pernicious.' It seems clear that Vivas does not anticipate much of value to come out of those alien societies which are composed of 'non-literates who are illiterate' (1961, pp. 51, 53, 56, 61).[5]

Nor has relativism been immune to sharp criticism from within anthropology. Of the variety of relativism propounded by Herskovits (1948), Murdock said 'not only nonsense but sentimental nonsense' (1965, p. 146). Freeman sees cultural relativism as an 'unscientific' doctrine of which we must rid ourselves if we are to develop a true science of man (1965, p. 65). Finally I. C. Jarvie, who dwells in the borderland between anthropology and philosophy, has found occasion to refer to 'the drab and nasty little idea called "relativism" ' (1968, p. 84).

Most curious of all, however, is that in recent years when anthropologists stop talking about what they have to teach students and other laymen and begin talking to each other, the notion of cultural relativism drops out of discourse almost entirely. For example, the cumulative index to the *American Anthropologist* for the decade 1959–69 lists a total of only four entries under 'cultural relativity' and 'cultural relativism.' The most substantial of these was a brief communication written not by an anthropologist but by a philosopher (Sylvester, 1959), while another was by a Jesuit missionary and dealt with Catholic moral theology rather than anthropological theory

(McManus, 1959). Since the third was a book review mentioning the inaptness of cultural relativism for applied anthropology and studies of development (Erasmus, 1967), we can perhaps appreciate Opler's point in the fourth (1968, p. 564): 'there has been an attempt to sweep cultural relativity under the rug in the interests of cross-cultural research and schemes for the uniform development of peoples.'

The climate of the times

Eric Wolf grounds the decline of ethical or evaluative relativism in the general development of anthropology and climate of opinion in the post-war world. He points to a shift in anthropological emphasis from cultural differences to cultural similarities and human universals (1964, p. 20) and to the rise of applied anthropology — an approach which clearly 'does not regard the culture that is applying anthropology as the equal of the culture to which anthropology is being applied' (1964, p. 24). A more general factor, he suggests (1964, p. 14), was the wartime mobilization, which

> made obvious the size of the gap that separated the anthropologist and the primitive. . . . No native who saw the masses of men and material that passed through the Pacific on the way to Japan could be in doubt regarding the differences in scale, in level of output and complexity, between his own culture and that of the foreign armies.

While the climate of opinion in the first decade or two after the Second World War may have been conducive to judgments that some cultures (like ours) are morally and intellectually superior to others, I think quite the reverse is the case in the 1970s. Consider the difference a decade can make. In 1961 Helmut Schoeck (Schoeck and Wiggins, 1961, p. 80), wrote that whenever he heard the relativist argument that we should allow

> social experimentation even with ideas such as socialism and communism for the possible benefit of our society. . . . I simply ask whether the speaker would wish a practicing, or at least a convinced polygamist to teach one section of the sociology course in marriage and family since, after all, that system is even more a happily 'going concern' in many parts of the world than

communism or socialism. I have yet to get an answer to that question.

One suspects that Schoeck moved in rather staid circles even for 1961, but certainly were he to pose his question in 1975 — when we have 'alternatives' to the conventional form of marriage at every turn — he would certainly receive the reply, 'Yes, by all means.'

How many thoughtful Americans would agree today with Redfield's conviction of two decades ago that mankind, with civilized nations such as ours in the van, is becoming more mature and humane? The last decade or so has been a period of national introspection in the United States, and our institutions have not weathered close scrutiny well. The civil rights movement and violence in Selma, Watts and Newark dramatized that racial inequality, the bigotry producing it and the frustration resulting from it, are far from dead. And significantly, even more than individuals, the culture as such has been indicted under the concept of institutional racism. The further realization that our institutions provide a less-than-fulfilling life for half the population has resulted in Women's Liberation, which in turn has spawned a multitude of 'alternatives': to marriage, to monogamy, to the nuclear family household, to the traditional sexual division of labor, and on and on. Incidentally, the very fact that 'alternatives' is such a popular concept these days in all areas ('alternatives to the classroom,' etc.) suggests to me a pervasive dissatisfaction with the traditional institutions of American society.

A rash of political assassinations and some mass murders have engendered concern that violence is deeply imbedded in American culture. Violence turned outward in the form of the war in Vietnam has fueled self-criticism more than any issue, and has even been held responsible for a national neurosis. You can easily think of more cases of trouble detected in American institutions: self-perpetuating creatures like the military-industrial complex and technocracy which are accused of enslaving and dehumanizing men, the implications of the Watergate scandal for the American political system, and so on.

While American institutions come under fire, those of other cultures are accorded increasing respect. Television advertisements pointedly compare our ultra-polluting society with the American Indian's fellowship with the environment. American blacks seek to build a separate identity which incorporates values derived from Africa; some variants of this movement explicitly reject Christianity in favor of Islam. Many young Americans enthusiastically follow various prophets and teachers from India. Even the fundamentalist Christian revival of Jesus freaks looks to another culture: an idealized image of a remote time when men lived in close-knit communities pervaded by simple and unshakable Christian faith.

Given all these considerations, it seems safe to say that the climate of the early 1970s in America is anything but conducive to the idea that our culture occupies a position of moral superiority in today's world or in history. What about intellectual superiority? Those who hold out for Western pre-eminence almost invariably point to science.[6] Especially in its technological and industrial application Western science is clearly superior — a fact people from other cultures admit as readily as we do.

But this is far from encompassing the entire spectrum of human experience and inquiry. The Indian who aims to merge his existence with the absolute or the wounded Zande who, while acknowledging that it is the nature of lions to attack occasionally, wants to know why that particular lion clawed *him* — these find far more satisfying answers in their own cultures than in scientific knowledge imported from the West.

Moreover, there is evidence that in contemporary America people are becoming more concerned with precisely those questions for which science offers no answer. The empirical world — home ground for science and technology — seems to be less satisfying today than a decade or two ago. People seek to escape it for some other, more intense, level of experience via psychedelic drugs, mystical religious experience, transcendental meditation, the ecstasy of the Hare Krishna cult, even an intensified experience of inter-personal relations produced by non-verbal communication in encounter groups and other techniques associated with Esalin Institute, or the sense of total trust and sharing in the ideal commune. Anthropological evidence of this search for non-empirical reality is the enormous popularity of Carlos Castaneda's books about the Yaqui sage Don Juan (1968, 1971, 1972). This popularity — enough to warrant a cover article in *Time* — may be due to the fact that 'Don Juan's teachings have reached print at precisely the moment when more Americans than ever are disposed to consider "non-rational" approaches to reality' (*Time*, March 5, 1973, p. 36).

Even within the academic and scientific community there are developments which jeopardize the role of science as the privileged avenue to truth. One is Thomas Kuhn's view of a science as a sequence of paradigms, with its implication that science is evolving out of earlier science but not necessarily *toward* anything we can call absolute truth (1962, pp. 169–70). Another is the news that acupuncture really works — even though it springs from a theory of anatomy, physiology and medicine radically different from our scientific one.

Hence, while not denying the material achievements of Western science and technology, it does appear to me that the climate of the times inclines toward relativism in intellectual as well as moral issues. People in our society today are open to the possibilities that truth may dwell in realms other than the empirical, that it may be found by modes of inquiry other than the scientific, and that the most satisfying answers to questions of greatest importance to them may be provided by cultures other than our own. Perhaps this general shift of opinion accounts for a revitalized concern with relativism in the anthropology of very recent years. Following his statement quoted above about relativism having been swept under the rug, Opler went on to predict: 'Still the tell-tale lump remains to embarrass the hostess. I look to a housecleaning one of these days that will make it possible to utilize this important concept again' (1968, p. 564). That relativism once more arouses interest is attested by Tennekes's book (1971) devoted to the subject, extended treatment by Needham (1972, pp. 160–246) and the numerous other references cited in the present work.

Comparison and development

Murdock faults cultural relativism on two major counts. For one, he sternly takes Benedict to task for the notion that any cultural element can be understood only in the context of the total culture to which it belongs (Murdock, 1965, p. 146, see also Jarvie, 1970, pp. 240–4). Such an attitude, claims Murdock, is destructive to comparative studies. For another, he rejects Herskovits's point that, given the equal validity and dignity of all cultures, no evaluation should be made across cultural boundaries. Murdock rejects it because everywhere he sees people valuing foreign goods higher than the materials of their own culture (1965, pp. 149–50).

All people reveal a preference for steel over stone axes, for quinine and penicillin over magical therapy, for money over barter, for animal and vehicular transportation over human porterage, for improvements in the food supply which enable them to rear their children and support their aged rather than killing them, and so on. They relinquish cannibalism and head-hunting with little resistance when colonial governments demonstrate the material advantages of peace. Such evidence indicates that different cultural adjustments to similar needs are by no means of equivalent utility or practical worth. Some must manifestly be superior to others in at least a pragmatic sense if they are always chosen in preference to the latter when both alternatives are available.

Murdock places such choices at the heart of social change and development, and argues that a relativist anthropology geared to the unique totality and pristine quality of each culture ill prepares us to study these important processes. Relativism is rather part of the anthropological conservatism which hopes to arrest social change and to maintain 'human zoos' of cultural difference available for our study (1965, pp. 146–7). Murdock's interests lie elsewhere: 'What we urgently need is systematic scientific knowledge about the choices for change which people do and do not make when presented with an opportunity, the criteria according to which such decisions are made, and the modes of implementing them effectively' (1965, p. 150).

In these opinions, Murdock has an ally in Ernest Gellner, who assaults especially that brand of relativism purveyed by Peter Winch (1958, 1964).[7] Gellner points to the rapid diffusion of Western science and industry in all parts of the world as indisputable evidence that 'the cognitive and technical superiority of one form of life is so manifest, and so loaded with implications for the satisfaction of human wants and needs — and, for better or worse, for power — that it simply cannot be questioned' (1968, p. 405). I have acknowledged the cross-culturally accepted technological superiority of Western civilization, and would only caution that we do not expand this to a claim of general superiority for our culture. As I have argued above, choices that people in our society now make for things like Indian philosophy and religion, astrology and witchcraft over ways of believing and knowing more conventional in our culture are strong evidence against such a generalized claim.

Since the Murdock-Gellner thesis of anti-relativism cannot defensibly rest on a claim of *general* superiority of some cultures over others, we must take it to hold that some cultures are better equipped to satisfy *some* human wants and needs than others. This view is entirely true, as the preceding paragraphs make plain. Yet, I do not agree that it can be taken as grounds for rejecting relativism. One can reach that conclusion only by obscuring the vital distinction between individual and institutional questions.

As noted in the previous chapter, Murdock's psychologically-oriented anthropology has tended to focus on individual questions. The passages quoted above are a case in point: there he is interested in the relative ability of institutions to satisfy human wants and needs. Gellner is obviously concerned with the same problem, and it is clearly one which calls for cross-cultural comparison and evaluation.

If individual questions like this one were the only kind one asks in social science, then Murdock and Gellner would indeed have a telling argument against relativism. But there is a great deal to know about institutions beyond their ability to satisfy people's wants and needs. One can also ask about their logical structure: the way they presuppose, imply, or contradict each other in a complex cultural system. These are what I have called institutional questions. Here relativism is the appropriate approach, for our concern is with the intrinsic, implicational meaning of cultural institutions. This, as I argued in the preceding chapter, is to be found by viewing institutions in their own terms — in their logical relation with each other.

Let me hasten to disavow any implication that each institution must be understood in the context of its *total* culture — a position which, as noted above, Murdock imputed to Benedict. Cultures are not so perfectly integrated or monolithically organized to merit such radical holism. For example, if one wishes to understand Rapan politics it is well to know about the church, the French colonial system, and the keeping of sheep (among other things), whereas fishing, the theory of disease, and the keeping of goats are less relevant to the subject (F. A. Hanson, 1970a, pp. 174–82). Moreover, the relativism I propose contains no claim that a culture is seamless, impervious to the outside world (see Jarvie, 1970, pp. 240–4). It is a simple fact that many of any culture's institutions are influenced by or derived from other cultures. I do hold, however, that like all institutions, imported ones should be understood according to their relations with other institutions *in the culture under study*. A custom or institution need not mean the same thing in a culture which has borrowed it as it does in its culture of origin.

Finally, institutional questions and the relativist approach suited to them are by no means unfitted for studies of development or the comparative method. We gain a deeper understanding of the meaning of institutions by tracing their development, while knowledge of the dynamic and changing relations among institutions materially enhances our understanding of social change. Institutional questions, for example, play important roles in Marx's dialectical materialist theory of history, Weber's thesis about the development of ascetic capitalism (1958), and Sorokin's (1941) views on the cyclical development of Western Civilization. Moreover, once their intrinsic meaning has been understood in its cultural context, there is nothing to prevent us from comparing institutions or patterns of institutions cross-culturally. Comparison from an institutional perspective is central to Wittfogel's (1959) theory about differences in the development of oriental and occidental civilizations. In the same vein, one might cite again Miller's (1955) comparison of Fox and European concepts of authority, and also my own comparative analysis of political change in Tahiti and Samoa (F. A. Hanson, 1973).

Ideological v. *methodological relativism*

Many recent discussions of relativism have been organized around a distinction between ideological and methodological relativism (Kaplan and Manners, 1972, pp. 5–6).[8] The point of this distinction is that we should use relativism as a tool to avoid ethnocentric distortion of alien customs, but that we should not extend this methodological prescription to the more pervasive ideological or philosophical position that cultures are incommensurable because of the uniqueness of each one, or that moral or ethical judgments must not be made across cultural boundaries. To my mind the way this distinction has been used is not strong on conceptual foundation. It seems just to be an *ad hoc* way of acknowledging relativism where it is obviously useful (don't judge African polygyny by our standards of monogamy) while conveniently ignoring the perplexing problems that relativism poses (what cross-culturally valid grounds do we have for judging the morality of genocide or abortion, or for determining the relative truth values of science, magic and mysticism?). I think critical issues such as these are brought more clearly to the fore when relativism is discussed according to the evaluative and epistemological problems it raises, as is being attempted in this chapter and the next.

Perhaps distinctions between philosophical and methodological relativism can be contrasted most clearly with the analysis advanced in this book in the following way. In each case, the effect is to limit cultural relativism well short of the extreme implications sometimes claimed for it. This limitation, however, is achieved in different ways. Philosophical/methodological distinctions take relativism as a unitary doctrine which, while useful in moderation, should not be taken too far. The analysis of this book divides cultural relativism into two corollaries: evaluative and epistemological. It then achieves the limitation by arguing that the evaluative corollary is spurious and (the task of the next chapter) by trying to be as clear as possible about what can be meant by epistemological relativism. Viewed in this light, the analysis presented here has much less in common with distinctions between philosophical and methodological relativism than with a distinction like Wolf's (1964, pp. 21–2) between cultural and moral relativism. My distinction between epistemological and evaluative relativism parallels his, and we are in agreement that moral or evaluative relativism is not tenable. One of the main differences between us is that he reaches his conclusions via an examination of the intellectual climate of post-war anthropology whereas I reach my similar ones through an exploration of the logic of relativism.

Chapter 3

Understanding other cultures*

Having argued that the thesis of cultural relativism properly has no evaluative corollary, we come to the epistemological side of relativism. This is the idea that cultural phenomena should be understood from within, in their own terms. The intrinsic meaning of Navajo witchcraft, for example, lies in its relations with other Navajo institutions and hence should be understood in terms of those institutions rather than against criteria drawn from alien sources such as Western science or Zande witchcraft.[1]

It should be apparent by now that the notion of understanding other cultures internally is fraught with baffling difficulties; in fact, the very possibility of achieving such understanding is clouded by doubt. In this chapter I want to argue that these problems stem not from the peculiarity or complexity of the subject matter with which social science deals, but rather from our way of *thinking* about that subject matter. If we alter that way of thinking, the problems connected with penetrating alien cultures will not appear so hopeless.

The problem connected with understanding an alien culture internally has two facets. One concerns the nature of the beliefs, customs, institutions to be understood: are they intrinsically of such rationality or intelligibility as to be comprehensible to us? The other

* This chapter is based on an essay I wrote in collaboration with Rex Martin (Hanson and Martin, 1973).

focuses on the process of understanding which should take place in us: what sort of cognition and other experiences must we undergo before we are justified in claiming that we understand elements of a foreign culture internally? Most people who have written about the epistemological aspect of relativism tend to consider it in terms of one or the other of these questions, so it will help our discussion if we treat them separately, at least at the beginning. What I have to say about the rationality of alien institutions can be said fairly briefly, so I will turn to that facet of the problem first.

Cross-cultural rationality

The epistemological corollary of relativism, that other cultures be understood from within, would appear to imply that alien beliefs, norms, and other institutions should be understood according to the standards of rationality and intelligibility of their own cultures. In so far as those standards are different from our own, relativism would appear to counsel 'a temporary suspension of the cognitive assumptions of our own society' (Peel, 1969, p. 82), presumably to make room for the categories and assumptions of the society under investigation. The best known recent argument tending toward such a relativist stance is that of Peter Winch in *The Idea of a Social Science*. Embracing a Wittgensteinian perspective, Winch holds 'that criteria of logic are not a direct gift of God, but arise out of, and are only intelligible in the context of, ways of living or modes of social life. It follows that one cannot apply criteria of logic to modes of social life as such' (1958, p. 100). It also follows that one cannot legitimately judge the rationality of what is done in one mode of social life against criteria of logic drawn from another. As for intelligibility (1958, p. 102):

the philosopher will in particular be alert to deflate the pretension of any form of enquiry to enshrine the essence of intelligibility as such, to possess the key to reality. For connected with the realization that intelligibility takes many and varied forms is the realization that reality has no key.[2]

Now certain advantages of cultural relativism are readily apparent. For instance, in the example already cited the refusal of Rapans to drink cold water when hot and perspiring, initially puzzling to us, makes sense when it is seen in the context of Rapan ideas that such an act may upset the temperature equilibrium within the body and hence produce disease. But when relativism becomes so total as to include issues as fundamental as the very standards of rationality and intelligibility, it seems to cut us adrift from any anchorage in firm knowledge whatsoever. After all, how could we count a belief or practice as rational if it is such only according to standards of rationality foreign to our own? Or how could we understand an element of another culture if it is unintelligible by our criteria of intelligibility?

Questions like these are corrosive to the whole enterprise of anthropology for they cast doubt on the very possibility of cross-cultural understanding. Small wonder that they have sparked a lively debate among anthropologists and philosophers.[3] Baffling as this problem may seem, however, I will argue that it is only apparent and stems from confusion about the words we use. When one becomes clear about what these words mean, particularly 'rational' and 'irrational,' the problem simply vanishes.

As an example of confusion clouding these words, consider the following passage concerning a particular interpretation of the Eucharist: 'If it is taken as metaphorical or false or without truth-value or irrational, then it is unintelligible' (Hollis, 1968, p. 244). It is not clear whether Hollis considers the words separated by 'or' to be different alternatives or near-synonyms. But certainly this passage says that an irrational belief is unintelligible; beliefs which are false or metaphorical are also seen as unintelligible (and perhaps also irrational). It is anything but helpful to weld such diverse meanings into a single unit![4] I may consider the Ptolemaic geocentric theory of the universe to be false, but that does not necessarily render it irrational or unintelligible. The notion of an electric current is metaphorical, modeled on hydraulics, but this does not impeach its truth-value, rationality, or intelligibility.

So the first step in dealing with the question of whether standards of rationality and intelligibility vary between cultures is to be ab-solutely clear on what we mean by the rationality or irrationality, intelligibility or unintelligibility of alien beliefs and customs. One effort in this direction is Jarvie and Agassi's discussion of the rationality of magic. 'Let us attribute rationality to an *action* if there is a goal to which it is directed; let us attribute rationality to a *belief* if it satis-fies some standard or criterion of rationality which has been adopted, such as that it is based on good evidence, or is beyond reasonable doubt, or is held open to criticism, etc.' (1967, p. 55, their italics). Jarvie and Agassi go on to argue the thesis that while science is rational in the 'strong' sense of people acting rationally on the basis of rational beliefs, magic is rational in the 'weak' sense of people acting rationally (their acts are goal-directed) but not on the basis of rational beliefs.

Jarvie and Agassi's discussion is disappointing. First of all, while the definition of rational action is straightforward enough, their definition of rational belief will scarcely do. We are given no guidelines for applying the criteria specified: what evidence is 'good'? When does doubt become 'reasonable'? What constitutes legitimate criticism? Remember that this definition applies to foreign beliefs as well as our own. So whose answers do we accept for these questions — ours, or those of a native of the society from which the belief comes? And finally, the definition actually *defines* (determines the boundary or limits of, lays down definitely) nothing at all because it ends with the open-ended term 'etc.'! Which standards of rationality, foreign or domestic, does 'etc.' admit and which does it rule out? Jarvie and Agassi's definition fails to provide any clear notion of what can be meant by the rationality of alien beliefs.

In fact, Jarvie and Agassi's approach actually deflects attention away from this entire issue. For them, 'the really urgent sociological problem posed by magic' is not so much 'what do magical acts mean' as 'can people with inefficient magical beliefs come to be critical of them, under what conditions and to what extent?' (1967, pp. 62, 74). The problem they pose is certainly an interesting one, but it is quite distinct from the issue of if and how beliefs can be understood as rational across cultural boundaries. Nothing testifies more eloquently to the poverty of Jarvie and Agassi's approach with reference to that issue than the fact that their only response to the question of why people in some societies perform magic is completely blind to the logic or meaning of magical beliefs and practices. Instead, they reply that people who perform magic think it can help them achieve their goals — a truism which has never been questioned by anybody (see Beattie, 1970).

Another, more successful, attempt to be clear about what can be meant by the rationality of alien beliefs and actions is that of Steven Lukes (1967). He distinguishes between two kinds of criteria of rationality: 'universal' criteria which 'simply *are* criteria of rationality' in any and all contexts, and 'context-dependent' criteria which 'are to be discovered in the context in which they are held' (Lukes, 1967, p. 260, Lukes's italics). Thus, if we encounter a belief which initially appears irrational, such as the famous Nuer proposition that twins are birds, it is probably not rational by universal criteria but at the same time we may discover and specify the context-dependent criteria according to which the belief is rational in its particular setting. In its essentials this position is shared by Hollis (1968, pp. 241–4) and Beattie. As the latter put it with reference to ritual beliefs: 'while we may regard such beliefs as irrational in the sense that they are not of the same order as the empirically-grounded and testable hypotheses of science (or "common sense"), they are by no means irrational in the sense that they lack coherent organization or a rationale. The associations and classifications which they involve, like those in music, drama and the other arts, may make perfectly good sense — though not "scientific" sense — when they are understood' (Beattie, 1970, p. 257).

Consider first the universal criteria of rationality. Lukes provides no explicit list of what he takes them to be, but it is fairly certain that 'the concept of negation and the laws of identity and non-contradiction' (1967, p. 261) are to be included for starters. With these purely formal criteria I have no quarrel. Yet these quite clearly do not exhaust Lukes's universal criteria. As far as I know, for example, the propositions involved in Zande magic, the Rapan hot-cold theory of health and disease, and Christian theology (with the possible exception of a few mysteries like the doctrine of the trinity) do not violate the canons listed above, and yet Lukes would be unwilling to accept them as universally rational (or 'rational (I),' as he calls it). In fact, it seems that about the only things he will accept as entirely 'rational (I)' are common sense and science. Concerning other things he writes: 'in so far as primitive magico-religious beliefs are logical and follow methodologically sound procedures, they are, so far, rational (I); in so far as they are, partially or wholly, false, they are not' (1967, p. 262). Clearly, then, *truth* is to be added to Lukes's list of universal criteria of rationality. And what he means by 'true' in the universal sense is quite clear because he denies that status to beliefs 'which do not satisfy rational (I) criteria in so far as they do not and could not correspond with "reality"': that is, in so far as they are *in principle* neither directly verifiable nor directly falsifiable by empirical means' (Lukes, 1967, p. 263, his italics).

This is where I disagree. I can see no justification for removing the criterion of truth just described from any particular context and maintaining instead that it is applicable and valid in any and all contexts. To hold this is to deny the plain fact that there exist many areas or contexts of human activity in which empirical verifiability and falsifiability is simply irrelevant: the Hindu sage seeking union with the Absolute, the Quaker seeking and heeding his 'inner light,' the composer or poet creating a work of art, even the mathematician working in the arithmetic of the transfinite cardinals. And it is equally plain that empirical verification does apply in a particular, definable context: one limited to activities relating to material reality. But I repeat, that is but one of many contexts in which human beings operate, albeit one which certainly occupies at least some precincts of every human culture. Empirical verification is a context-dependent criterion in that particular arena; it is not a relevant measure of truth, rationality or meaning in other contexts of human activity.[5] So far as I can see, universal criteria of rationality should be limited to purely formal criteria such as non-contradiction and the others listed above.

Turning now to context-dependent rationality, I want to suggest that reasoning via this concept we can find a solution for the problem of the rationality of alien beliefs and actions. As we originally posed that problem on the basis of some passages from Winch, it led to a mind-boggling epistemological impasse: how can we conceive of beliefs and behavior in another culture as rational if they are such only according to standards of rationality different from ours? But if we reflect on what can be meant by 'rational' in this sentence, we find that it is Lukes's context-dependent sense of rationality. And further reflection reveals that the context-dependent concept of rationality boils down to nothing more or less than *meaning*. As Beattie put it, magical behavior has 'a rationale, that is, a meaning (or meanings) in terms of the symbolic ideas of the people concerned' (1970, p. 249). Moreover, it is the kind of meaning that emerges from the relations between beliefs, from the organization of beliefs and customs in a pattern or system. In a word, the 'rationality of alien beliefs' is nothing other than their *implicational meaning*, as that concept was developed in Chapter 1.[6]

Hence we see that the question of the rationality of alien beliefs poses no baffling epistemological problem at all. The question actually concerns the *meaning* of those beliefs, and that is perfectly intelligible to us. We determine it by ascertaining the relations among those beliefs, how they presuppose and imply each other in a logical system. The only set of beliefs which would qualify as non-rational or meaningless by this reasoning would be one in which the component beliefs vary randomly, with no logical connections between them at all. I doubt very seriously that such a 'system' (better, nonsystem) of beliefs could exist for long in a human society.

The passages from Winch with which this section began mentioned intelligibility as well as rationality. So let me close it now with a word on intelligibility. As with rationality, the question of intelligibility can be posed in a baffling way: may not alien beliefs be simply unintelligible to us because they are intelligible only according to standards of intelligibility different from our own? And again as with rationality, this is an unfortunate, fruitless and confused way of looking at it. Actually the issue of intelligibility can be broken into two questions. The first is, are alien beliefs intelligible to us at all? That is, can we understand them *in any way*? This question can be dealt with quickly; the answer is simply 'yes.' Our reasoning here runs together with that we followed for the rationality question: alien beliefs are meaningful in the sense that they are linked by relations of implications. When we understand those relations, we understand the meaning of the beliefs; they are intelligible to us. The other question is, can we understand alien beliefs *in the same way the natives understand them*? This would seem to be necessary if our understanding is to be internal, as the doctrine of cultural relativism demands. Hence we arrive at the other facet of the epistemological problem connected with cultural relativism which I noted at the start of this chapter: what sort of cognitive and other experiences must we undergo before we are justified in claiming that we understand a foreign culture internally? This is a complicated problem, and the rest of this chapter is devoted to untangling it.

Internal understanding

We will launch our analysis of internal understanding with an example drawn from my study of Rapa. I found that most Rapans would like to limit their families to two or three children. To this end they practice a rhythm method of birth control, but they find it most ineffective. 'I don't understand it,' remarked one woman, then expecting her eighth child. 'We abstain from intercourse for three or four days right after my period every month, but I keep getting pregnant!' My wife and I suggested that they might have better luck if they abstained for a week or more midway between menses. She looked at us oddly, plainly unconvinced. Further checking revealed it to be the general opinion on Rapa that conception occurs during the few days immediately following menstruation. We argued that this view was mistaken but to little avail; when my wife's unanticipated pregnancy with our first child became known shortly thereafter, it did not foster confidence in our contentions. At any rate, here is a belief drawn from an alien culture and, on the face of it, unintelligible to us. How can we understand it, internally?

Several months passed before we gained such understanding. Then we realized that Rapan location of the fertile period is quite reasonable in the light of their ideas about the anatomy and physiology of conception. Rapans do without ova, ovaries and fallopian tubes. In their view conception occurs in the uterus, the result of the mingling of womb-blood and semen. If conception does not occur, stale blood is expelled each month in menstruation, to be replaced with a fresh supply. Menstruation ceases upon conception, because all the blood entering the uterus is used to build the foetus. The uterus is conceived to be a mechanical organ which opens and closes. Remaining tightly closed most of the time, it opens for several days each month to allow the stale blood to run out. Rapans support their concept of a mechanical uterus with their belief that blood is harbored in the uterus in liquid form, like water in a bottle. If the uterus did not open and close but remained perennially open, they argue, then instead of regular menstrual periods there would be a constant seepage of blood. These mechanics of the uterus explain the Rapan placement of the fertile period. Just as blood cannot escape a closed uterus semen cannot enter it, so there is no possibility of conception during the greater part of the cycle. (Hence one can understand their incredulity at our assertion that conception is most likely to occur about midway between menses.) Conception could occur during menstruation but ideas that menstrual flow is contaminating lead them to avoid intercourse at this time. However, the uterus remains open for a few days after menstruation, and this is the time when, in Rapan eyes, conception occurs.[7]

Now that we know their anatomical and physiological premises, we can readily understand the Rapan belief about when the fertile period occurs. Moreover, this understanding qualifies as internal because we follow the Rapans' own reasoning, moving from their premises to their conclusion. Hence as a first approximation we may state that internal understanding involves a *duplication* of native mentality — grasping the native point of view, sharing their inner thoughts, being able to go through their reasoning in one's own mind.[8] Understanding in this sense has been advocated by Dilthey under the name *Verstehen* (Rickman, 1960; Tuttle, 1969, pp. 8–9), by Collingwood (1946, pp. 215, 283, 296–8) and Dray (1957b, 1958) as 're-enactment' or 're-thinking,' and by many others.[9] It rests on the ability to establish empathy with one's subjects — which is one reason why anthropologists value long periods of fieldwork by participant observation.

Psychological validity

As long as natives are aware of why they do and say things, and can explain it, internal understanding poses few problems. For example, although it took a good deal of inquiry to get them out, all of the anatomical and physiological ideas and the reasoning about conception recounted above were told to us by Rapans. Nothing in that example comes from my inference. Hence we can be sure that the reasoning we go through duplicates Rapan thought, and therefore that in this case our understanding is indeed internal. Very often, however, people can give no satisfactory account of the inner motives or rationale for why they say or do certain things. Consider another example, again from my Polynesian research. On Rapa, anyone who is sick, pregnant or lactating observes a prohibition against eating octopus, lobster, and fish from the deep sea (tuna, salmon, etc.). I quizzed numerous Rapans about this taboo, but no one could give me so much as a hint of a rationale or set of rules behind it. This is an example of behavior which is rule-governed in Winch's (1958, p. 64) sense that people can say whether or not it is being done correctly, although they cannot formulate the rules they follow. Another example is language. Millions of people are capable of speaking grammatical English and of pointing out mistakes, but are utterly unable to express rules for their usage; even professional linguists have yet to encompass the language with an adequate set of rules. Here the notion of internal understanding encounters a serious difficulty: how can we understand internally the activities, judgments, and beliefs of people who can offer no satisfactory criteria, rules or rationale for them?

A common procedure is to conceive of such beliefs or behavior patterns on the model of explicit ratiocination. One assumes, that is, that the decision a Rapan makes to avoid certain foods while sick, pregnant, or lactating is reached in much the same way as a decision to abstain from intercourse for a few days after menses. In both cases the natives are thought to apply certain rules or criteria in some logical process. The difference is that in the latter case the reasoning is conscious while in the former it occurs at the subconscious level and the only part of the process that emerges in the conscious mind is the conclusion. From this point of view the investigator's mandate is to lay bare the entire process: to infer from observable statements or activities the concealed criteria and logic that produced them. This seems to be the rationale behind Wallace's statement that in the analysis of a foreign system of classification, 'the question is whether the anthropologist is able not only to predict which objects will be referred to by which terms but also to predict what criteria the native speaker will employ in determining the appropriate term to use.' And this comes after he has acknowledged that the native application of such criteria may be 'latent or perhaps unconscious' (1965, p. 231). Once the investigator has determined the subconscious rules or criteria he can achieve internal understanding because he can duplicate the natives' cognitive process. He can put himself in their place and retrace consciously the ratiocinative transit which his subjects presumably negotiate unawares.

But this procedure is scarcely satisfactory because it raises a problem of verification: how can the investigator be certain that he has inferred the *right* rules? As the concept has been developed up to this point, for understanding to be internal it is necessary to *duplicate* native cognition, and the process of inference set out above provides no guarantee that this has been achieved. This is what in anthropology is known as the problem of psychological validity (Burling, 1964; Wallace, 1965). It is usually possible to infer more than one set of rules which can accurately generate a classification of kinsmen, diseases, plants, or whatever is under study. Leach (1958) and Lounsbury (1965) championed rival rules for the Trobriand kinship system; in a single paper Burling (1965) worked out two alternative sets of rules for generating Burmese kinship terminology. So which of the schemes devised by the investigator — if any — is the one the people really use, and which are mere functional equivalents? As Burling wrote, 'It certainly sounds more exciting to say we are "discovering the cognitive system of the people" than to admit that we are just fiddling with a set of rules which allow us to use terms the way others do. Nevertheless, I think the latter is a realistic goal, while the former is not' (Burling, 1964, p. 27).[10]

Appeal is sometimes made to basic cultural similarities between the investigator and his subjects as grounds for thinking that his inferences about their subconscious minds are accurate. But that is clearly remote from a tough-minded procedure of verification; nor can it be of comfort to the medieval or ancient historian or the anthropologist, who require conceptual tools suited to cultures radically different from their own. For these scholars problems like psychological validity seem to render internal understanding simply impossible. As Danto colorfully put it, 'I have no internal understanding of what it is like to believe that Prester John is saving souls in Ulan Bator; for I am unable, in the light of my other beliefs, either to hold this belief myself or to imagine how the world would look to one who truly believed it' (1966, p. 572). He continued that internal understanding 'will carry one to forms of life similar to one's own only insofar as they are similar, and, where similarity breaks down, external understanding alone remains possible' (Danto, 1966, p. 575). And from Berlin (1954, p. 61): 'the modes of thought of the ancients or of any culture remote from our own are comprehensible to us only in the degree to which we share some, at any rate, of their basic categories.' Similar sentiments have been voiced by many others, including Collingwood (1946, pp. 300, 307–8, 329), Troeltsch (Stark, 1958, p. 199), Walsh (1967, pp. 33–4) and Weber (1947, p. 104; Parsons, 1965, pp. 53–4).[11]

Hence the problem of psychological validity, especially when aggravated by cultural difference, brings the enterprise of internal understanding to an abrupt halt. I will not attempt to solve the problem here; indeed, within the framework of the discussion of internal understanding above I do not think it can be solved satisfactorily.[12] Nor do I think, however, that this represents a fatal weakness in the idea of understanding other cultures internally for I will argue that there is another way of conceptualizing internal understanding in terms of which psychological validity is no problem at all. The crux of the issue lies with the concept of mind. Notice how phenomena of mind have been constantly at the center of discussion in the preceding pages. Our concern has been with native motives, explanations, rationales, and with natives' experience of their beliefs — all mental phenomena. I shall argue that what one considers internal understanding of alien cultures to be depends very largely on what he considers mind to be.[13] First I will show how the traditional concept of mind generates the concept of understanding which founders on the problem of psychological validity, and then I will suggest how an alternative theory of mind enables us to avoid that problem.

Cartesian dualism

What I have called the traditional theory of mind is most commonly associated with Descartes. While it has been called 'the dogma of the ghost in the machine' (Ryle, 1949), a more neutral label (and the one I shall henceforth use) is Cartesian dualism.[14] In essence, this theory holds that each man has a body and a mind. All of a man's overt, public activity — walking, talking, eating, writing, and so on — are activities of his body. Mental activities on the other hand are 'internal.' They take place in his mind — some metaphorical 'place' hidden deep within him. The activities of his mind include his planning, calculating, scheming, musing, dreaming, loving, sorrowing — in short, all his thoughts and emotions.

This bifurcating theory has two corollaries of importance to us. First, it is asserted that most bodily activities are caused by mental activities. One raises his arm, leaves the room, recites a poem or makes a particular point in discussion because he has decided to do so. Thus the activities of mind and body usually go tandem with each other, with mental activities pushing off first. So when someone is delivering an argument or writing an essay, the words are chosen first in his mind and then produced in the physical world via his tongue or his hand and pen.

The second corollary, known as 'privileged access,' relates to the ways in which mental and bodily activities are known. The activities of the body occur in the external world and are open to direct public inspection. Anyone can perceive what a man is doing with his hands by looking, and what he is saying by listening. But activities of a mind are directly available only to the possessor of that mind, by means of introspection. Others have no way of directly apprehending what he is thinking or feeling. To be sure, there are signs which give clues to what is going on in the mind. If you are laughing your mind is probably enjoying something funny, if your brow is furrowed you are probably pondering, if you are crying you are probably sad — although without more evidence one could make no guess as to *what* it is that you find humorous, puzzling, or dispiriting. But none of these is a case of direct inspection of the contents of your mind. They are all indirect modes of knowing, being only inferences from some of your bodily activities. In other words, we can know, or reasonably believe, that there are certain internal mental events that lie behind the bodily activities we have observed; but we could know for certain what these are only if we could experience these inner workings for ourselves.

It can readily be seen that the concept of internal understanding previously described stems from a Cartesian theory of mind. First of all, that concept of understanding urges the analyst to penetrate through overt sayings and doings in order to get to the hidden rules, thought, feelings, and emotions. And this is because, according to Cartesian dualism, the real action is on the inside. Public words and deeds are mere results of private, inner motives, drives, plans, feelings; these hidden workings of mind are the true objects of our study. In effect, this view represents an extension of what Chomsky said about language to culture as a whole (1968b, p. 23, see also 1968a, p. 7):

> The person who has acquired knowledge of a language has internalized a system of rules that relate sound and meaning in a particular way. The linguist constructing a grammar of a language is in effect proposing a hypothesis concerning this internalized system.

Again, on the theory we have been examining, to understand alien thought is to re-enact or duplicate that thought in one's own mind. This too results from Cartesian premises. The Cartesian view is that one knows the contents of one's own mind directly, by introspection, while one has no direct access to the contents of other minds. This doctrine, however, leaves one chink in the wall that otherwise bars one from direct knowledge of other minds. If only one could get the contents of someone else's mind into his own mind, then he could know these thoughts directly, by introspection. And this is the rationale behind the whole idea of understanding by re-enactment, or *Verstehen*. One may know, by direct introspection, the thoughts and beliefs of another by literally duplicating them as something he experiences in his own mind (see Dilthey, 1962, pp. 124–5 and, for criticisms, Ryle, 1949, pp. 56–7, Gardiner, 1952, pp. 126–8).

Finally, the problem of psychological validity also stems from Cartesian dualism, especially from its doctrine of privileged access. That theory of mind tells us that expressed beliefs and observed patterns of behavior in other cultures are merely the results or effects of hidden activities of native minds. Our true objective is to understand those mental activities, by recreating or re-enacting them in our own minds. But how can we know for certain that the thoughts we 're-enact' in fact *are* the thoughts entertained by the natives? Privileged access, which denies the possibility of direct apprehension of the contents of other minds, renders it impossible to verify whether we are 're-enacting' the natives' thoughts or mere functional equivalents. Hence Cartesian dualism ultimately takes away with one hand what it proffers with the other. It lays down a concept of internal understanding and at the same time decrees that it is impossible ever to achieve this, given the doctrine of privileged access and the problem of psychological validity it spawns. This is the dead end where the concept of internal understanding discussed thus far expires, unfulfilled.

Clearly something is wrong here. What is needed is an approach to other cultures which does not require us to deny the possibility of achieving the very kind of understanding it recommends. Since the source of our troubles has been identified as the Cartesian theory of mind, perhaps replacing it with another concept of mind would remove many of the difficulties.

Ryle's concept of mind

An alternative to Cartesian dualism has been available since Aristotle; the philosophers in our century who have been foremost in advocating it are Ludwig Wittgenstein and Gilbert Ryle (A. White, 1967, pp. 46-55). Here we shall rely mainly on Ryle's presentation of the theory in *The Concept of Mind*.

For someone accustomed to thinking in Cartesian terms it requires a radical shift to appreciate Ryle's theory, for he adamantly denies the notion that mind is limited to a hidden, inner theater where private acts are performed. Instead he brings mind into the open, including among its activities many deeds which would be classed as workings of the body from a Cartesian perspective (Ryle, 1949):

> Overt intelligent performances are not clues to the workings of minds; they are those workings. Boswell described Johnson's

mind when he described how he wrote, talked, ate, fidgeted and fumed [p. 58]. To talk of a person's mind is not to talk of a repository which is permitted to house objects that something called 'the physical world' is forbidden to house; it is to talk of the person's abilities, liabilities, and inclinations to do and undergo certain sorts of things, and of the doing, and undergoing of these things in the ordinary world [p. 199; see also p. 168].

Thus tying one's shoe, observing table manners or forming grammatical sentences are not merely public *results* of clandestine activities of mind. They *are themselves* activities of mind, the kind that Ryle calls 'overt intelligent performances.'

This should not lead one to conclude, as it has led some, that Ryle insists that *all* activities of mind are overt. He readily acknowledges what is obvious to anyone: that one can rehearse a sentence silently before speaking or writing it; can 'hear' a tune, do a problem in arithmetic, or indulge a daydream 'in one's head' without anyone else being aware of it. Ryle's argument is with those who insist that these interior goings-on are the sole and quintessential stuff of mind, who draw a sharp *logical* distinction between what is private and what is public in their theory of mind. Ryle's position is simply that there is no radical difference between 'hearing' a melody in one's head and humming or whistling it aloud, doing a piece of addition silently and whispering (or shouting, for that matter) the sum as one works, or rehearsing a sentence silently and muttering it under one's breath before writing it down. Ryle holds that these are activities of the same sort, activities of mind; some just happen to be done aloud or publicly and others in silence or privately.

So Ryle is not saying that a person never has private thoughts or, when he does have them, that he has no special advantage in discerning them. But he is saying that having access to private goings on in a mind (one's own) reveals nothing that is *in principle* different from what he could find out by examining overt doings, on his own part or on the part of others. Moreover, what one finds out privately is not immune from error and must be understood exactly as he understands the public sayings and overt conduct of other people (Ryle, 1949, pp. 40, 61). Private access is not privileged access.

This discussion of the philosophy of mind was undertaken in order to argue that Ryle's theory enables us to conceive of understanding other cultures internally without falling prey to the baffling problems that plague the Cartesian concept of internal understanding. Let us now turn specifically to that point. First, Ryle's concept has a distinct advantage over Cartesian dualism for the understanding of alien belief systems, in that it brings the workings of other minds out of inaccessible places. As A. J. Ayer said of Ryle's theory: 'It saves us from the difficulty, to which all dualistic theories are exposed, of explaining how mental and physical processes are related or how one person can ever come to know what goes on in the mind of another' (1970, p. 55).

Actually, I do not think that the two theories would differ at all in an initial statement of what internal understanding of another culture means. For both, it means to grasp the native point of view, to be able to duplicate or re-enact native reasoning and other mental activities. But here is the critical point of divergence: since the two concepts of mind are at odds over what mental activities are, to duplicate them means quite different things in the two theories.

Cartesian dualism holds that activities of mind are limited to private, inner theaters. Hence, to understand native beliefs in Cartesian terms is to duplicate in the recesses of one's own mind that which is occult and privately going on in native minds. And that, as we have seen, is the Achilles heel of the Cartesian theory because, given the presumed cultural differences together with the doctrine of privileged access, it is highly unlikely (and in any case impossible to verify) that one could achieve the sharing or duplication necessary for understanding.

By contrast, Ryle's theory of mind holds that most mental activities are open to public view: they are overt intelligent performances. If understanding thought in another culture means sharing native mental activities, in Ryle's terms this would mean being able to duplicate native overt intelligent performances. It is much the same as when we say that one knows or understands a foreign language when he can use it; in Ryle's terminology, understanding is a case of *knowing how* (Ryle, 1949, p. 54, his italics).

> A spectator who cannot play chess also cannot follow the play of others; a person who cannot read or speak Swedish cannot understand what is spoken or written in Swedish; and a person whose reasoning powers are weak is bad at following and retaining the arguments of others. Understanding is a part of *knowing how*. The knowledge that is required for understanding intelligent

performances of a specific kind is some degree of competence in performances of that kind.

The core of Ryle's theory of understanding, then, is not communion of private experiences (based ultimately on an inner/outer distinction) but rather one's ability to do or use something. Wittgenstein shares this concept of understanding: 'Let us remember that there are certain criteria in a man's behavior for the fact that he does not understand a word: that it means nothing to him, that he can do nothing with it' (1968, I, section 269, see also sections 150–5, 421). And Waismann set down an especially lucid statement of this position (1965, p. 349):

> There are certainly symptoms by which in everyday life we are guided in distinguishing between a genuine and a pretended understanding. These symptoms — and this is the important point — refer without exception to the further use of the word. If one therefore asks 'Do you understand this word?', this question is much more like 'Can you operate with this word?' than like 'What experiences do you have when you hear this word?'

There is nothing the least bit unusual or curious about this concept of understanding. In fact, we use it constantly. For example, when in a discussion or an examination we wish to satisfy ourselves about a student's understanding of some theory, we do not concern ourselves as to whether he goes through the same process of reasoning as Darwin did when developing the concept of natural selection, or whether he has the same feelings and experiences as Einstein did when contemplating the perihelion of Mercury. Our concern is exclusively with how well the student can operate with the theory: his ability to present it cogently and reasonably, to show logical connections between its various parts, to apply it to bodies of data, intelligently to criticize it. If he can successfully perform tasks such as these, we conclude that he understands the theory.

Rules

But the whole issue here is cultural relativism — the notion that our understanding of other cultures should be internal. Doubtless knowing how amounts to understanding of some sort, but are we willing to admit that it is *internal* understanding? The argument can easily be made that it is not. Knowing how does not come of itself; it results from the application of rules. For example, while learning a foreign language one manages to form grammatical sentences only by the laborious application of rules. It is the same in learning to use unfamiliar ways of thinking, alien manners and customs, and so on. Natives also conform to rules, although they are so practiced that they do not do it consciously and are often unable to articulate the rules they follow. The critical question concerns the relation between their rules and ours. If in learning how to do what they do we follow rules *different* from those the natives use then while knowing how would count as understanding of some kind, it certainly would not be *internal*. Thus we run again into the problem of psychological validity.

One response to the psychological validity problem is to dismiss it as spurious because of its assumption that there is only one psychologically valid set of rules. On the contrary, hold Wallace and others, different natives themselves operate according to different subconscious rules, so that rules which are psychologically valid for some natives may not be so for others (see Wallace, 1962, 1970, pp. 29–36; Goodenough, 1971, p. 15; Sanday, 1968, p. 522). I agree with the conclusion that the problem of psychological validity is spurious, but for reasons different from theirs. My argument will be that the psychological validity problem is absurd because it rests on muddled thinking about the nature of rules. Once that point is made, I will go on to argue that Ryle's notion of 'knowing how' does indeed constitute internal understanding in the only meaningful sense of that term.

What can it mean, precisely, to say that of alternative sets of rules, one gets the subconscious processes of one or more natives 'right' (i.e., it is psychologically valid) whereas another does not? It cannot mean that the former successfully accounts for observed behavior while the latter does not, because all of the sets of rules in question are functionally equivalent — they generate the same prescriptions for action. It must mean that the psychologically valid rules are a true rendition of the native's subconscious thinking; they are the *same* as the rules that he applies subconsciously. But remember that rules of the 'psychologically valid' analysis are propositions or imperatives which exist in words and are linked logically. To hold that the native follows the same rules is to assume that in his subconscious mind he goes through those very propositions (or translations of them in his own language) and those precise logical steps.

But surely that is taking a conscious, ratiocinative model of the subconscious mind too literally! Bluntly put, whatever is 'in' the subconscious mind, it is not a bunch of propositions, and it therefore cannot be literally duplicated by propositions (see Spradley, 1972, pp. 8–18, 25–7). Hence it is simply absurd to think that the propositions and logical steps of our analyses could ever duplicate subconscious cognition, for they are a different kind of thing.

If not one of identity, just what is the relation between the native's subconscious rules and the rules of the anthropologist's analysis? I suggest it is that which Mario Bunge set out in his discussion of scientific laws. In one sense, 'law' means an objective relation or pattern in nature. Such laws exist in objective reality, in the sense that regularities or patterns exist, but certainly not in the form of propositions or verbalizations of any sort. When the scientist writes down or says what he knows of a law, that statement is also called a 'law.' Here, however, the word 'law' is used in a different way. The scientist's formula or sentence is not itself the objective pattern or relation in nature; it is a *statement of* that pattern or relation, a rendering of it in verbal form. Bunge labels 'law' in this sense a 'law-statement.' Thus the objective pattern of moving objects (a pattern which, in nature, does not exist in words or mathematical symbols at all) is the law of mechanical motion. The various 'laws of motion' which have been advanced by scientists, such as Aristotle's law 'force equals resistance times velocity,' Newton's law 'force equals mass times acceleration,' or Einstein's law 'force equals the rate of change of momentum' are *law-statements* which express the law more or less accurately (Bunge, 1959, p. 95).

In precisely the same way, the rules which appear in our analyses are *statements of* the rules subconsciously applied by the natives. Viewed in this light, the psychological validity problem is unmasked as absurd. It is not that, of alternative, functionally equivalent sets of rules, only one can be 'right' (psychologically valid) and the others must be 'wrong.' Being a different kind of thing, the rules which appear in our analyses do not and cannot literally duplicate the natives' subconscious rules. Instead, they are simply different ways of *stating* or *formulating* those subconscious rules. In so far as they account equally well for observed behavior, they are equally 'right.'

Having thus disposed of the psychological validity problem, how can we now characterize internal understanding? As I see it, internal understanding amounts to this: when the natives can tell us the rules they follow, their rationale for acting, we understand their behavior in those terms. When the natives cannot articulate the rules they follow, we make formulations or statements of them by inference, statements which we evaluate by their ability to account for or predict behavior which natives accept as appropriate. And from this point it is easy to see that internal understanding as just defined is equivalent to 'knowing how,' because the critical test is always our ability to *use* the body of custom or system of thought under study. It is to know the correct moves, to know what natives would accept as appropriate responses in particular circumstances.

One other important point of equivalence must be recognized: to understand cultural institutions internally is nothing other than to know their implicational meaning, as that concept was defined in Chapter 1. To understand institutions internally is to know how to use them, and to know how to use them is to know how institutions relate to each other — the way they presuppose, imply, contradict, co-exist with each other; how one move calls for or rules out another. And finally, the way that institutions relate to each other is precisely what I have called their implicational meaning. Hence internal understanding of cultural institutions is knowing their implicational meaning.

This point is of critical importance to our discussion of cultural relativism. The present chapter began with all kinds of paradoxes and problems lurking around the idea of understanding an alien culture internally. But the analysis has shown that those problems are just artifacts of our usual way of conceptualizing internal understanding — notably, via Cartesian dualism. Another way of looking at it, from Ryle's perspective, dissolves the paradoxes and problems in the simple and straightforward solution that internal understanding is a matter of knowing how. To understand another culture internally is not to undergo certain feelings or experiences nor to recapitulate subconscious native cognition in our own minds. Instead, it is knowledge of the implicational meaning of that culture, the way its institutions are logically organized, through a process which takes full account of native explanation and extends beyond native exegesis via our own inference of principles or rule-statements. It is a disciplined process wherein accuracy is checked throughout by assessing the quality of our 'knowing how,' the degree to which our analysis enables us to use or operate with the institutions under investigation in ways which natives would accept as proper. I suggest that this procedure generates internal understanding in the only viable sense of that term. Together with the last chapter's conclusions on evaluative relativism, this concept of internal understanding constitutes what I promised would be a 'critical redefinition' of cultural relativism.

Synopsis

My presentation of the logic of institutional questions in social science is now essentially complete. It may be useful at this point to recapitulate the main features of the argument.

1 The empirical reality with which all social science deals consists of human behavior and its products — the things people do, say, make, or arrange. These may be called human phenomena.

2 Unlike natural things, human phenomena are intrinsically meaningful.

3 The goal of social science is to make the intrinsic meaning of human phenomena intelligible.

4 Human phenomena can be approached in different ways; we can ask different questions of them.

5 One common class of questions concerns why people engage in certain kinds of behavior. Because these questions focus mainly on persons, they are labeled individual questions.

6 Answers to individual questions reveal the *intentional* meaning intrinsic to human phenomena. They specify the intentions, reasons, drives, needs which motivate or stimulate people to act.

7 Another common class of questions concern the things that people do and say — customs, beliefs, theories, etc. — in their own right. Because these questions focus on patterns of behavior or elements of culture, they may be called institutional questions. This book is primarily concerned with institutional questions.

8 Answers to institutional questions reveal the *implicational* meaning intrinsic to human phenomena. They specify the logical relations of reinforcement, contradiction, or simple co-existence among the various institutions of a culture.

9 The implicational meaning of any institution is to be found in its relation to other institutions of the same culture. Therefore the institutional study of any culture should be from within; a culture should be understood in its own terms. This is the doctrine of cultural relativism.

10 Cultural relativism does *not* imply that we must evaluate the truth or morality of alien institutions in their own terms. It does imply that we should internally understand indigenous evaluations. But an evaluation can be ours only if we affirm the criteria on which it is based, and understanding foreign criteria by no means necessarily entails affirming them to be good or true. *Our* evaluations are based upon *our* criteria.

11 Internal understanding does not imply that we somehow grasp alien beliefs and behavior as rational according to standards of rationality that we do not share, or as intelligible according to criteria of intelligibility which are not our own. In this usage of the term, 'rationality' is equivalent to 'meaning.' Hence we understand the rationality of alien beliefs when we understand their implicational meaning. In so far as they are not random they have such meaning, and therefore they are intelligible to us.

12 Nor does internal understanding mean sharing natives' inner experiences and re-enacting natives' private thoughts. That concept of understanding, generated by Cartesian dualism, leads to baffling problems such as psychological validity.

13 Adopting Ryle's concept of mind, internal understanding becomes a matter of 'knowing how' — knowing how to use beliefs, ideas, manners, customs like the natives use them.

14 We are able to use alien institutions through the application of rules. Those rules are statements of the patterns, relations and regularities which exist among the institutions of the culture under study.

15 Therefore understanding alien institutions internally by knowing how is equivalent to knowing the implicational meaning of those institutions, because in both cases the focus is on logical relations among institutions. Hence the cultural relativist position that alien institutions should be understood internally does not imply that one's understanding should be accompanied by certain feelings or experiences. Instead, as these concepts are construed here, to understand alien institutions internally is neither more nor less than to know their implicational meaning.

Further remarks

Probably the most stubborn obstacle in the path of understanding other cultures internally is the problem discussed above under the rubric of psychological validity. This is the question of how we can be certain that our understanding is internal in the sense of accurately duplicating or specifying the clandestine cognition which imputedly moves in subconscious native minds. In the main text of this chapter I moved rapidly through (better, around) the psychological validity problem in order to come directly to the stance I advocate regarding internal understanding. Now I want to amplify the problem somewhat and discuss a few previous attempts to solve it.

As for the problem of psychological validity itself, it is exacerbated by Max Weber's point that regardless of how objectively our investigations are carried out, our own values inevitably enter into the selection of subject matter, into the very questions we ask (Weber, 1949, pp. 81–2, Parsons, 1937, p. 594).[15] Convincing evidence of how the investigator's presuppositions and questions condition his findings may be seen in Richards' (1967) contrast between the approaches of French and British anthropologists to African systems of thought.

As noted already, one response to the psychological validity problem is to hold that internal understanding is possible only in circumstances of cultural similarity between investigator and investigated. Such a view is by no means confined to the philosophical deliberations of scholars; it is closely tied to the extremely widespread tendency in contemporary society to think that knowledge stems much more from experience than from analysis. How many times in recent years has it been said, for example, 'You can't understand black people unless you are black yourself?' Again, in a recent television documentary about the Mafia, a young man was asked how the Italian-American community felt when Joe Colombo was shot. The reply was, 'Unless you are Italian yourself, there's no way you can understand how we feel.'

Probably the clearest instance of the popular concept of knowledge as experience is the notion of vibrations (see Moody, 1971, p. 285). This is a whole world view, often associated with the counter-culture, which holds that everything and everyone in the universe emits a particular kind or frequency of vibrations. Knowledge is not a matter of study or learning, but of harmonious vibrations. One understands intimately (can 'relate to') things and people with vibrations which resonate harmoniously with one's own, while remaining ever a stranger to those people and things with discordant vibrations. Affinities between the theory of vibrations and the question of psychological validity, with its Cartesian overtones, are scarcely surprising. In the last analysis there is not so much difference between the notion of harmonious vibrations and the Cartesian notion of internal understanding as the sharing of clandestine, subconscious cognition.

Ideal types and 'as if'

One important attempt to deal with the psychological validity problem is Weber's concept of ideal types. For Weber, understanding in sociology is a matter of knowing the 'subjective meaning' of acts and artifacts, which is to say their relation to an 'intended purpose' (Weber, 1947, pp. 88–93). But Weber acknowledges that agents are often not aware of the subjective meaning of their acts (1947, pp. 111–12).

> In the great majority of cases actual action goes on in a state of inarticulate half-consciousness or actual unconsciousness of its subjective meaning. . . . Only occasionally and, in the uniform action of large numbers often only in the case of a few individuals, is the subjective meaning of the action, whether rational or irrational, brought clearly into consciousness.

Weber goes on to argue that this difficulty (1947, p. 112)

> need not prevent the sociologist from systematizing his concepts by the classification of possible types of subjective meaning. That is, he may reason as if action actually proceeded on the bases of clearly self-conscious meaning. . . . It is often necessary to choose between terms which are either clear or unclear. Those which are clear will, to be sure, have the abstractness of ideal types, but they are none the less preferable for scientific purpose.

That is, Weber invites the social scientist to hypothesize subjective meaning, or intended purposes, and to proceed *as if* people acted with such purposes explicitly in mind — although we know full well that in fact people act for the most part out of impulse or habit and with no clear realization of the subjective meaning of what they do. Weber's proposal has the ring of a last-ditch operation, a desperate endeavor to make a silk purse of systematic and elegant analysis out of the sow's ear of actual human behavior. It is hard to see how anyone would opt for an approach resting on acknowledged fiction unless one had despaired of making any sense out of the reality of human action.

I suggest that Weber was driven to this unfortunate position[16] because he failed to recognize the approach to human affairs via institutional questions and their answers in terms of implicational meaning. That failure is clear in *The Theory of Social and Economic Organization*, where he identified subjective meaning with 'intended purpose' and explicitly argued that subjective meaning is to be found only in 'the behavior of one or more *individual* human beings' (1947, pp. 93, 101, Weber's italics). From these beginnings one inevitably ends up with a fictional or 'as if' approach: if you insist that human action is to be understood in terms of the intended purposes of the agents and yet you find for most actions the agents can articulate no clear intentions, you have very little choice except to make up intentions yourself (ideal types) and to proceed as if the agents operated according to them.

An approach quite similar to Weber's is that used by Jacques Maquet. He is reluctant to attribute anything to a culture which is not explicitly known to members of that culture: 'Only an expressed world view may be said to constitute a cultural philosophy; implicit philosophies are useful constructs devised by an outside observer, but they are not part of the social heritage of the observed society' (1964, p. 17). This implies a strong dose of 'as if' in one's theoretical orientation. Hence Maquet says of his own analysis of Ruanda (1964, p. 17, Maquet's emphasis):

> the principle of inequality does not belong to the culture of Ruanda: it is a logical inference drawn from observed facts by an anthropologist. . . . Ruanda people behave *as if* they believed in the fundamental inequality of men and wanted to translate this belief in their social relations.

Again we are led to the unhappy conclusion that social science is largely an enterprise of fiction, devoted to building castles in the clouds. The castles may be useful and enlightening, but they are no more substantial for that fact.

Problems which in Weber's and Maquet's method call for fictitious ideal types lend themselves better to analysis from an institutional perspective. Here there is no need to fabricate the meaning we seek by insinuating fictitious purposes into agents' minds, because the intentional meaning of agents is largely irrelevant to institutional questions. Instead, the meaning sought is of the implicational variety — the ways in which the beliefs, behavior patterns and other institutions agents use articulate with each other. Ruanda *people* may not have the slightest inkling of a 'premise of inequality.' Still, that principle expresses the reality of Ruanda *culture* in that it states part of the intrinsic, implicational meaning of Ruanda institutions. Because implicational meaning is really there, in the logic or structure of institutions, our analytical statements are not ideal types in the sense described above. There is nothing fictitious or 'as if' about them.[17]

Situational logic

Now I should like to examine a few approaches to explaining human action to which my approach bears some similarity. One is situational logic. Associated primarily with Karl Popper, it has been expounded in print at greatest length by Popper's loyal student I. C. Jarvie (1964, 1972). Briefly, situational logic holds that human affairs are to be understood according to (1) people's intentions and (2) the unintended consequences of their acts (Popper, 1963, pp. 95–7).

Unpacking that brief characterization, the first part holds that people have intelligible ends and that they act 'rationally faced with their situation, where "their situation" includes their knowledge and beliefs' (Jarvie, 1964, p. 36). That is, we are to understand someone's behavior in terms of his goals, intentions or reasons and in the context of his view of the situation. As for the great many human phenomena which are not intelligible in terms of the reasons or intentions of individuals, these are unintended consequences and they should be understood in their own right (Jarvie, 1972, p. 43).

> Primarily [the social sciences] are concerned to explain typical, repeatable and unintended phenomena and hence to gain an understanding of the society in many ways totally different from the understanding we would attribute to its members. . . . Unreflective social living is not the concern, but abstract and theoretical grasp of the working of social structures and institutions.

The approach of this book has much in common with situational logic, in that the latter's dual focus on intentions and unintended consequences is paralleled by my distinction between individual questions (which ask about intentional meaning) and institutional

questions (which concern implicational meaning). It is especially
interesting to compare Popper's concept of unintended consequences
with mine of implicational meaning. His fullest treatment of the
logic of unintended consequences is found in some recent and excellent papers on the 'third world' of 'objective mind' (Popper, 1968,
1969).[18] There he argues that knowledge in the objective sense (i.e.
systems of ideas, such as a scientific theory) should be studied in its
own right. One understands the development of a science, for
example, according to its initial problem situation, the theories
advanced in response to that problem situation, the consequences of
such theories (unforeseen and unintended by their authors) for new
problem situations, the development of new theories to cope with
them, *their* unintended consequences for still other problem situations, and so on. Expand these remarks to encompass cultural
institutions of all sorts, and one is in the realm of what I have called
institutional analysis. In that event, one could speak of the unintended consequences, not only of ideas for other ideas but also of
forms of social and economic organization, political movements,
ethical and aesthetic values for each other. This is probably the kind
of analysis Jarvie has in mind when, as quoted a moment ago, he
speaks of an 'abstract and theoretical grasp of the working of social
structures and institutions.'

From this perspective the concepts of unintended consequences
and implicational meaning emerge as remarkably similar, for both
concern logical relations among institutions and social conditions
which are not, or not necessarily, recognized by natives. Still, there
are different nuances between them, such that our tool kit for institutional analysis is richer if we keep both concepts rather than
trying to banish one in favor of the other. 'Unintended consequences'
seems particularly tuned to the effects of some concrete event or
process. It has a clear sequential — even causal — connotation: the
consequences come *after* the original event or development and are
effects of it. 'Implicational meaning,' for its part, concerns how
institutions and developments are linked, not so much to concrete
events or processes, as to abstract principles or axioms of culture. It
connotes little of the temporal sequence and causal direction of
unintended consequences: it draws attention more specifically and
exclusively to logical consistency (or the lack of it) among institutions
and developments.

Given these variations of meaning, certain cases are more aptly analyzed via one of these notions rather than the other. For instance, unintended consequences would be the more appropriate concept for use in a theory of history which relates the development of capitalistic industrialization to the formation of an oppressed, dissatisfied and potentially revolutionary urban proletariat. On the other hand, implicational meaning would be the more fitting concept to use if one wished to demonstrate how the theory of history just mentioned, the idea of progress, the theory of evolution, the Christian notion of a world that was created, fell from grace, was redeemed and will be destroyed, and just about any other Western concept of history all exemplify a basic Western presupposition that time is linear. Despite these divergent nuances, however, the concepts of unintended consequences and implicational meaning overlap in large measure and can often be used interchangeably.

There is, however, another aspect of situational logic that disturbs me. It is that its adherents stoutly claim it to be anti-relativist. Why this should be I cannot fathom. Some of the arguments advanced are remarkably facile, as where Popper suggests that communication across cultural boundaries can be enhanced if only people would 'give up cocksureness, and become open to criticism' (1963, p. 387). Surely the basic issues of relativism run deeper than cocksureness! Moreover, as I see it situational logic is itself a relativist approach. Jarvie directs us to understand people's intentional behavior in the context of their view of the situation (1964, p. 36) — a relativist prescription. As for unintended consequences or 'objective mind,' Popper urges understanding of things like scientific theories in the context of the 'problem situations' from which they emerge (1968, pp. 37–9)[19] — also a relativist recommendation. Moreover, when expanded to include institutions other than the intellectual, Popper's 'third world' becomes coterminous with culture. Similar expansion of his point about problem situations results in the relativist counsel that all institutions should be understood in their own cultural context. Hence I find it curious that Popper & Co. oppose relativism so strenuously when, as far as I can see, relativism is at the core of situational logic.

Certainly this problem is more semantic than substantial, for the Popperians and I must not mean the same thing by 'relativism.' Probably my relativism remains too extreme for Popperians in that I do not elevate truth over meaning (Popper, 1969, pp. 245–6) and am reluctant to speak even of '(absolute) truth' (Popper, 1969,

p. 248) or of how things really are as opposed to how people see them (Popper, 1968, p. 40). But as to the precise reaction which my concept of relativism would evoke from Popper or his followers, I do not venture to guess.

Rational explanation and individual questions

Very similar in some respects to situational logic is the approach which William Dray calls 'rational explanation.' A rational explanation is one which 'gives what we should normally call the agent's *reason* for acting as he did, . . . which displays the *rationale* of what was done' (Dray, 1957a, pp. 123–4, Dray's italics). This, of course, is consonant with that aspect of situational logic which holds that people act rationally, given their view of the situation (Jarvie, 1964, p. 36). And what Louch terms 'moral explanation' is essentially the same thing (Louch, 1966, p. 4):

> When we offer explanations of human behaviour we are seeing that behaviour as justified by the circumstances in which it occurs. Explanation of human action is moral explanation. In appealing to reasons for acting, motives, purposes, intentions, desires and their cognates, which occur in both ordinary and technical discussions of human doings, we exhibit an action in the light of circumstances that are taken to entitle or warrant a person to act as he does.

The similarities between these concepts of explanation and *Verstehen* or Collingwood's notion of understanding by re-enactment are manifold, in that we can understand an agent's action as reasonable or warranted only if, given his view of the circumstances, we can share the agent's view that it is a rational or appropriate thing to do. Indeed, Dray explicitly derives his concept of rational explanation from Collingwood's theory of re-enactment and draws no major distinctions between them.

The first point to make about rational explanation is that it does not represent complete explanation of human phenomena. In the phraseology of this book, rational explanation is concerned exclusively with individual questions and intentional meaning: not at all with institutional questions and implicational meaning. As we have seen, the latter are recognized in situational logic via the concept of unintended consequences. In fact, Popper criticizes Collingwood and Dilthey, among others, for seeing the third world of objective mind in terms of the second world of consciousness (Popper, 1968, pp. 29, 45–6) — that is, for dealing with institutional questions in individual or psychological terms.[20]

Another limitation of rational explanation and other concepts of the same species would seem to be that they are applicable only to acts which are 'thought out' by the agent — a general's strategy, Caesar's crossing of the Rubicon, an architect's design. Perhaps we may speak of people having motives of which they are not aware, but it does not seem to be proper usage to say that people act out of reasons, intentions or purposes of which they know nothing. The limitation to explicitly planned behavior is especially clear with reference to Collingwood's notion of understanding thought by re-enactment, for how can we 're-enact' thought that was never 'enacted' in the first place (see Gardiner, 1952, p. 49; Gruner, 1967)?

This criticism assumes that re-enactment theory and rational explanation rest on the Cartesian premise that overt actions stem from internal activities of mind. Dray (1958, p. 203; see also Dray, 1957b), however, is quick to deny Cartesian dualism. He makes his point with reference to Collingwood, whom he claims

> would agree with Ryle and Wittgenstein that having a certain thought is not, in essence, a matter of reciting certain propositions to oneself, or focusing certain images on one's internal cinema screen, or 'going over' in any such way what one is about to do. The being of a thought is in its expression; and thoughts are expressed in actions as well as in those internal monologues and private screenings which are associated with reflecting and planning.[21]

Hence for Dray there is nothing to prevent us from understanding by rational explanation those actions not preceded by the agent's explicit planning (1957a, p. 123, his italics).

> Indeed, it is tempting to say that in such cases there is *no* calculation to be *re*constructed by the historian. But such an admission need not affect the main point; for in so far as we say an action is purposive at all, no matter at what level of conscious deliberation, there is a calculation which could be constructed for it: the one the agent would have gone through if he had had time, if he had not seen what to do in a flash, if he had been called upon to account

for what he did after the event, etc. And it is by eliciting some such calculation that we explain the action.

Yet even if the agent need not actually have gone through the calculation, it is clear from this passage that rational explanation is limited to actions for which the agent *could* provide a satisfactory rationale. It is not applicable to actions for which the agent does not realize or misunderstands his actual motives, nor to that part of behavior which consists of following cultural rules that the agent cannot formulate. In this latter area particularly, institutional analysis with its focus on implicational meaning represents a step beyond rational explanation in the study of human phenomena.

Chapter 4

But is it scientific?

Having set out the parameters of institutional analysis, we must now ask whether it is scientific. It is not a simple question. The answer depends on what one thinks science is, and there are several schools of thought on that point. In this chapter we will examine a few of those schools. In the process I hope it will become clear that while institutional analysis may not qualify as scientific according to certain distorted or truncated views of science, it does emerge as thoroughly scientific according to the fullest and most accurate conception of what scientists actually do.

Behaviorism and logical positivism

Institutional analysis is a means of making human affairs intelligible by investigating the structure or organization (implicational meaning) of the beliefs, norms, customs, behavior patterns represented in the actions one observes. The hallmark of institutional analysis is the attempt to give that structure or organization a general expression, in which a wide variety of institutions are seen as implications of a relatively few presuppositions or organizational axioms. Such high-order presuppositions are inferred by the analyst. One should not expect natives to volunteer them, nor necessarily even to understand or accept them if explained to them. Hence institutional analysis aims to go beyond or behind observed phenomena.

Its focus on meaning and readiness to go beyond observable reality immediately put institutional analysis at odds with certain highly empirical concepts of science. Marvin Harris, a cultural materialist, holds that any concern with native mentality or meaning is 'totally alien to the spirit of science' (Harris, 1964, p. 91). A similar point of view is expressed by Jones (1971, p. 172) in his attempt to apply the premises of behaviorism to anthropology.

Harré and Secord point out that the conception of science informing a behaviorism like Skinner's rests on a Humean concept of cause and a mechanistic model of man. On this model, people are viewed 'as mechanisms that, like less complex physical objects, respond to the push and pull of forces exerted by the experimenter or the environment' (Harré and Secord, 1972, pp. 30–1). According to Hume, one kind of event is thought to cause another if the latter regularly occurs after the former. The focus is entirely on the constant conjunction of observable events. No attention is paid to *how* events of one kind produce events of the other. Taken together, the Humean conception of cause and the mechanistic model of man result in a social science in which the investigator seeks to identify regularities between what happens to an organism (a pigeon, a rat, a man) and the behavior that the organism emits. Reasoning from within such a social science, 'it is obvious that the mind and the ideas, together with their special characteristics, are being invented on the spot to provide spurious explanation. A science of behavior can hope to gain very little from so cavalier a practice' (Skinner, 1953, p. 30). It is obvious that institutional analysis, with its focus on the intrinsic meaning of human phenomena, does not fare well by these criteria of science.

Another influential thinker who seems to operate according to the Humean notion of cause is the logical positivist Carl Hempel.[1] For him the *sine qua non* of science is the 'covering-law' form of explanation in which particular events are explained by subsuming them under general laws. One variant of such explanations is the 'deductive-nomological,' in which the laws are assumed to hold true invariably. Here is an example:

(a) This is a piece of sodium salt (an initial condition or assertion about a particular fact)

(b) Whenever a piece of sodium salt is put in a flame it turns the flame yellow (a general law)

Therefore

(c) When this piece of sodium salt was put in a flame, it turned the flame yellow.[2]

Hempel recognizes another kind of explanation utilizing covering laws, which he terms 'probabilistic.' Here the laws are expected to hold true with a certain statistical probability rather than invariably (Hempel, 1966b, pp. 100–3). This is the sort of explanation one would use, for example, in accounting for the drawing of a black ball from a box containing ninety-nine black balls and one white ball.

Covering-law explanations like these seem to presuppose the Humean conception of causality, in that they focus attention on the regular co-occurrence of observable events. They have been criticized by Toulmin (1966), Harré (1970) and others for not reflecting the actual practice of science, which is concerned not only with the existence of a regularity but also, and especially, with the (often unobservable) generative mechanism that *produces* the regularity. The scientist wants to know not only *that* sodium salts regularly turn flame yellow. He wants, especially, to know *why*: what it is about sodium salt that causes yellow color in flame (see Harré, 1970, pp. 274–5).

But to criticize Hempel in this manner misses the point, claims Nagel, for 'Hempel's main objective is to analyze the *logical structure* of scientific explanations rather than to examine the *process* of scientific discovery or the *development* of scientific ideas' (1966, p. 8, Nagel's italics). I think Nagel's clarification is extremely helpful. It helps us understand, for example, why Hempel is predominantly concerned with hypothesis testing, for it is that part of scientific investigation which lends itself best to expression in the form of deductive logic with covering laws. It also helps us understand Hempel's apparent allegiance to the Humean notion of cause, for it is entirely possible that the description of an experiment may involve no explicit reference to the hypothesized generative mechanism which that experiment was designed to test. For example, one may be investigating the notion of dominant and recessive genes in reproduction. A test relevant to such an investigation can be expressed in classical Hempelian fashion as follows:

(a) John has type AB blood.
(b) Mary has type O blood.

(c) Whenever a person with type AB blood mates with a person
     with type O blood, their offspring will have type A blood or
     type B blood, but never type O or type AB blood. (This is the
     covering-law.)

Therefore

(d) Any offspring of John and Mary will have blood types A or
     B, but never types O or AB.[3]

The critical point here is that while the above represents a test
relevant to a theory about a generative mechanism involving entities
and concepts like dominant and recessive genes, homozygotes and
heterozygotes, nothing about that theory is stated in the test conditions, covering-law, or conclusion. Hence it seems to me that
Hempel is not committed to a denial of the existence of generative
mechanisms, or even a denial that the search for such mechanisms
is an important part of science. It is simply that for the part of
the scientific enterprise to which Hempel turns his attention — the
empirical testing and confirmation of hypotheses — reference to
unobservable generative mechanism is not necessary.

This brings us to the most important conclusions we can draw
from Nagel's clarification of Hempel's intentions: because Hempel's
work in the philosophy of science relates to just one *part* of
scientific investigation, it does *not* provide adequate criteria for
determining whether a general program of inquiry is or is not
scientific. Hempel does indeed set out the scientific procedures of
hypothesis confirmation and prediction, and his ideas will be relevant
when we discuss these procedures in institutional analysis later in
this chapter. But to get started on the answer to our question of
whether institutional analysis is scientific, we had better turn to a
philosophy of science which covers a different part of scientific
praxis than Hempel's does.

Realism

We can find what we are looking for in the 'realist' philosophy of
science developed, among others, by Norwood Hanson (1958),
R. Harré (1970), Mary Hesse (1966), Thomas Kuhn (1962), Karl

Popper (1968, 1969) and Stephen Toulmin (1953, 1966). Let me hasten to acknowledge that these philosophers form a diverse assemblage who by no means agree with each other on all things. Moreover, the term 'realism' is notoriously polysemic in philosophy; even those philosophers listed above who use the term do not use it in the same way. But there is one point where they agree: when they philosophize about science they try to do so in the context of science as it is actually practiced. This is what Harré (from whom I borrowed the term) means by realism: 'the realist point of view in the philosophy of science eschews simplifications and tries to present a theory of science with some resemblance to scientific theory and practice' (Harré, 1970, p. vii).

From the realist point of view, 'scientific research consists both in the observation of the course of nature, both as to its regularities and irregularities, *together with* the persistent attempt to uncover the mechanisms from which both flow.' Again, 'it is the existence of the knowledge of, or the hypothesis of the model of, the generative mechanism that distinguishes the law-like conditionality of scientific statements' (Harré, 1970, pp. 27, 113, Harré's italics). In other words, the scientist is not only interested in the facts *that* sodium salts turn flames yellow or *that* offspring of parents with blood types O and AB respectively will have blood types A or B but never AB or O. He is also — and especially — interested in knowing *why* these events regularly occur. In answering that question the scientist commonly postulates or infers the existence of mechanisms in nature which are themselves unobserved but whose operation is taken to cause or produce the observable regularity he is trying to understand. Such inferences command the primary attention of realist philosophers, because most of them are interested in working out the patterns of scientific discovery, the logic of theory formation. This renders their work an antidote (or complement) to Hempel's focus on theory confirmation. It also makes the realist philosophy of science an ideal place to commence answering our question about the scientific status of institutional analysis.

A central element of institutional analysis is the attempt to understand the intrinsic meaning of human affairs. Harré and Secord, who set themselves to frame a realist philosophy of social science, are explicit that meaning is a proper object of investigation in the human studies, and that its investigation is entirely scientific (1972, pp. 9, 29, 39, 166, etc.). It is clear, however, that for the most part the meaning they have in mind is of the variety we have labeled intentional. Hence, while their work is excellent and of greatest importance for the analysis of individual questions, it is somewhat less relevant to our inquiry into institutional questions. Closer to institutional analysis is Popper's notion of the 'third world' of 'objective knowledge' — and in recent articles (1968, 1969) he stresses that its study is entirely scientific.

To the voices of Popper and Harré and Secord, I want to add my own argument for the proposition that institutional analysis is indeed scientific. Near the beginning of this book we noted the point of thinkers like Dilthey and Collingwood that human events differ from natural events in that the former have intrinsic meaning while the latter do not. One consequence drawn from this is that the methods of natural science are not appropriate to the human studies. As we pursued the notion of meaning in human affairs, however, we found it necessary to distinguish between two of its senses: intentional meaning and implicational meaning. The meaning to which Dilthey and Collingwood referred was essentially of the intentional variety. We found that to be particularly suited to individual questions. The kind of meaning in play when one asks institutional questions, the major concern of this book, is implicational meaning. Now my argument is this. If the intentional sense of meaning is under discussion, Dilthey and Collingwood are correct that it is intrinsic to human events but not to natural events. People intend things but planets, molecules, organs of the body, cells do not. But if we are talking about implicational meaning, there is no fundamental difference between human and natural events. By this I do not intend to argue that we start talking about the 'meaning' of natural events. That would distort common usage, cause confusion, and I see no advantage in it. But I do intend to argue that when we talk about the 'order' of nature or the 'consequences' of natural events, terms very commonly used in that way, we are talking about essentially the same thing as when we speak of the implicational meaning of human affairs. From that point it will be but a short and simple step to claim that institutional analysis is scientific.

First regarding natural science, realist philosophers of science hold that the fundamental aim of science is to make nature intelligible, to discern its *order*. Anything which demonstrates a pattern or order among natural phenomena is regarded as a contribution to science — it is the sort of thing scientists try to formulate. 'The great unifications of Galileo, Kepler, Newton, Maxwell, Einstein, Bohr, Schrödinger and Heisenberg were pre-eminently discoveries of terse formulae from which explanations of diverse phenomena could be generated as a matter of course; they were not discoveries of undetected regularities' (N. Hanson, 1958, p. 109).

Such unifications are formulated by a process which Hanson labels 'abduction' or 'retroduction': '1. Some surprising phenomenon P is observed. 2. P would be explicable as a matter of course if H were true. 3. Hence there is reason to think that H is true' (N. Hanson, 1958, p. 86).[4] What is the relation between H and P? It is a *logical* relation, such that P is a logical consequence or *implication* of H. Hence scientific theory formation is a process of devising principles or premises from which observed phenomena can be logically generated. 'This kind of reasoning gave birth to modern theoretical physics, research within which might be described as observation statements in search of a premise' (N. Hanson, 1958, p. 108).

Precisely the same kind of procedure characterizes institutional analysis in social science. There the purpose is to make a culture (or parts of it) intelligible by demonstrating the order among the institutions which make it up. And there too that order is *logical* in nature, for institutional analysis aims to discern how beliefs, customs, forms of organizations and other institutions logically presuppose and imply each other. This, of course, is what we have termed their implicational meaning. The close relation between this and thinking in the natural sciences is highlighted when we recall Collingwood's logic of question-and-answer, which I have suggested as a model for institutional analysis. That logic, it will be remembered, calls for the establishment of a hierarchy of presuppositions which enables us to understand the answers advanced by a given thinker in terms of the questions *he* was asking. Adapted to institutional analysis, it is customs, concepts, patterns of behavior, norms, axioms of world view which take their places in the tree-diagram of questions and answers, presuppositions and implications. The aim of institutional analysis, precisely as in natural science, is to make the *order* of the system under study intelligible. That is, to fill in the higher-order presuppositions or premises, themselves unobserved but from which the institutions discernible in observed behavior flow logically, 'as a matter of course.'

Hence we see that, so far as patterns of discovery and theory formation are concerned, institutional analysis operates in the same way as the natural sciences and thus qualifies as a scientific mode of investigation.

Confirmation and prediction

Now we may return to procedures of hypothesis confirmation and prediction, to determine where institutional analysis stands when judged against that phase of scientific investigation. This entails also a return to Hempel's covering-law model, because it captures quite accurately the scientist's confirmatory procedure of deducing the empirical implications of a hypothesis and then experimenting to determine if those implications in fact hold true.

Note that scientific prediction — which also involves deducing the empirical implications of hypotheses or theories — uses precisely the same logic as confirmation. In fact, each confirmatory test involves a prediction, because the experiment proceeds to determine whether results predicted by deduction from the hypothesis in fact occur. Therefore, confirmation and prediction can be discussed together. In what follows, the focus will be on prediction. In that way we can pursue our question of whether institutional analysis is scientific in the context of what many have claimed is an endemic and fatal weakness of social scientific theories — their lack of predictive power.

Whenever the issue of prediction comes up, it is essential to be absolutely clear about predicting *what*. People often chide the social sciences — or breathe a sigh of relief — because they cannot predict 'human behavior'; that is, they cannot predict exactly what any man or everyman will do in given circumstances. But institutional analysis, at least, is not concerned to *explain* 'human behavior' in that sense, and therefore it cannot legitimately be expected to predict it. Institutional questions represent a perspective on human affairs which asks not precisely why any individual acts as he does, but instead asks how the beliefs, norms, customs, and other institutions of a culture are organized. The questions are of course related, for the behavior of any individual depends in large measure on the institutions current in his society. But the individual's behavior also depends on his personality and idiosyncrasies, his particular goals, his own calculation of the situation (which may involve miscalculations), his mood of that day and his whim of that moment. These matters are of interest when one asks individual questions; institutional analysis does not take them into account.

Since institutional analysis is not concerned to explain precisely how anyone acts in any circumstances, it is scarcely sensible to fault it for its inability to predict any and all acts of human behavior. But where, then, does its predictive power lie? Institutions are guides to behavior: beliefs and concepts figure in the definition and evaluation of situations, norms stipulate proper courses of action in various situations, customs lay down molds for the form of action, and so on. Hence, although institutional analysis cannot predict exactly what someone will do in given circumstances, it *can* predict what would be *appropriate* (by the standards of his culture) for him to do (see Harré and Secord, 1972, pp. 148, 160). That is, if we have a theory about the institutional structure of a culture we will be able to make predictions regarding whether a particular kind of affront appropriately calls for some kind of direct action against the offender, a complaint to some agency of social control, or no action at all; whether a certain set of symptoms should be met with an aspirin, a certain kind of diet, a visit to a diviner or other medical practitioner or a confession of sins; whether being confronted with a certain dish calls for the long, thin fork, the short, fat one, or the fingers; whether the report of a certain sort of miracle is appropriately met by the simple application of one of the tenets of dogma, an expansion of or addition to dogma, or the excommunication or burning of a heretic.

These remarks also apply to the confirmation of theories or hypotheses. Given a theory about the institutional structure of a culture and a relevant set of conditions, we can predict whether a certain action would be judged by natives as appropriate or inappropriate. The procedure fits Hempel's nomological form perfectly. For example, deduction from a certain theory about Rapan concepts of health and disease could yield the following experimental test:

(a) Te'ura is a Rapan who accepts his culture's concept of health and disease.
(b) Te'ura is asked if it is appropriate to drink cold water when hot and perspiring.
(c) Any Rapan who accepts his culture's concepts of health and disease and who is asked if it is appropriate to drink cold water when hot and perspiring will invariably (or with high probability) reply in the negative.

Therefore,

> (d) If asked whether it is appropriate to drink cold water when
> hot and perspiring, Te'ura will reply in the negative.

This specifies a prediction, which can be tested empirically by putting
the question to Te'ura and receiving an answer. If the prediction
holds true, this test serves as a piece of confirming or corroborative
evidence for the theory about Rapan concepts of health and disease
from which the experiment was deduced.[5]

To conclude, theories stemming from institutional analysis do
have predictive power and are susceptible to empirical corrobora-
tion. Hence to our earlier conclusion that institutional analysis is
scientific as far as theory formation is concerned, we may now add
that it also qualifies as science in the realm of prediction and theory
confirmation. So we arrive at last at the synthesis promised in the
Preface. After thinking carefully about what it means to study the
intrinsic meaning of human phenomena and about how the enterprise
of science actually proceeds, it has become clear that no antinomy
need separate idealism from positivism in social science. So far as
institutional analysis is concerned, at least, the investigation of the
intrinsic, implicational meaning of human affairs is a scientific
study.

Further remarks

In a recent book extolling the merits of an 'explicitly scientific'
archeology, Patty Jo Watson and her colleagues join numerous other
'scientifically oriented' archeologists in adopting Carl Hempel's
concept of science as their own (Watson, Le Blanc and Redman 1971,
pp. 3–4). In America, at least, the logical positivist philosophy of
science, particularly as expounded by Hempel, is very commonly
taken by social scientists as the final court for deciding the scientific
merits of their work. I think that is unfortunate because, although
Hempel's views are useful for the logic of theory confirmation,
confusion and distortion result when one attempts to apply them to
all phases of scientific investigation. Some of the difficulties Hempel's
concepts encounter in the social sciences will emerge from the following critiques of his treatment of rational explanation and of functionalism.

Hempel and rational explanation

Earlier we discussed the notion of rational explanation as set out by William Dray, whereby an action is explained by demonstrating the agent's reasons for acting as he did.[6] For Hempel, rational explanation is incomplete and inadequate because it does not explain conclusively that the action in fact occurred. Someone may have reasons for doing something but still not do it. To complete the explanation, Hempel insists on adding the condition that the agent is rational and the covering-law that any rational agent in the circumstances in question will always (or with high probability) perform the action. On these grounds Hempel claims that, when the missing but necessary elements are filled in, rational explanation conforms to his covering-law model (Hempel, 1966b, pp. 117–18). I will argue, via a few examples, that this move of Hempel's entirely distorts social scientists' efforts to understand and explain human action, because it deflects attention from the real object of investigation and focuses it on trivial issues.

Each year, at the beginning of the rainy season, the Pastoral Fulani of the African Sudan move their herds from the rich pastures of the southern part of their range to the sparser grasslands of the more arid north.[7] Why do they do that? Because in the rainy season tsetse flies, which had been confined to humid thickets and along rivers in the dry season, spread out over the plains and threaten to infect the cattle with sleeping sickness. Hence, the Pastoral Fulani's reason or intention for moving north is to protect their cattle from the tsetse fly. This would qualify as an example of rational explanation.

Hempel would argue that this is only an explanation sketch. It gives sufficient grounds for thinking that it would be *appropriate* for the Pastoral Fulani to move their herds north at the start of the rainy season, but insufficient grounds for asserting that they actually do it. What is missing, or taken for granted, is the *law*. The explanation can be formalized and completed in the following way:

(a) Tsetse flies spread over the southern plains in the rainy season, threatening to infect cattle with sleeping sickness.

(b) The drier northern plains are free of tsetse fly.

(c) The Pastoral Fulani are disposed to act rationally. (This is a condition unstated in the explanation sketch, but required in a full explanation.)

(d) Any cattle owner who is disposed to act rationally and who finds himself in conditions (a) and (b) will move his cattle north at the start of the rainy season. (This is the law.)

Therefore,

(e) The Pastoral Fulani invariably (or with high probability) move their cattle north at the start of the rainy season.

Hence, the explanation of Pastoral Fulani transhumance conforms to the deductive-nomological or probabilistic forms.[8]

The Hempelian treatment of the Pastoral Fulani seems harmless enough, although it may start a twinge of uneasiness — does it really get to the heart of what we are trying to explain? A second example will escalate that twinge into a real pain.

Consider again the Rapan theory of conception, discussed in Chapter 3, wherein the fertile period is thought to occur during the few days immediately following menstruation. Assume that we observe (or are reliably informed) that a Rapan woman, Tiare, regularly avoids sexual intercourse for three or four days following menses. If we ask her why, she says she doesn't want to get pregnant. That would amount to an explanation sketch, which could be amplified in the same manner as we did for the Pastoral Fulani, as follows.

(a) Tiare does not want to get pregnant.
(b) Tiare is disposed to act rationally.
(c) Any rational woman who does not want to get pregnant will avoid intercourse for three or four days after menstruation.

Therefore,

(d) Tiare invariably (or with high probability) avoids intercourse for three or four days after menstruation.

If we were Rapans, affirming their theory of conception and aware of no other, that account would probably be acceptable. But we are not, and it is clearly not satisfactory to us. This points up an important matter regarding 'rational explanation': in a given set of circumstances there is not always just *one* appropriate or rational step to take. What is rational can vary with one's belief, with the construction one puts on the circumstances. Of course, this is not disastrous for Hempel's scheme. We can take account of the fact that Tiare's beliefs about conception differ from ours by fixing up the conditions and law in the explanation:

(a) Tiare does not want to get pregnant.
(b) Tiare believes that pregnancy is likely to result from sexual intercourse during the first three or four days after menstruation.
(c) Tiare is disposed to act rationally.
(d) Any rational woman who holds the aim (a) and the belief (b) will avoid intercourse for three or four days after menstruation.

Therefore,

(e) Tiare invariably (or with high probability) avoids intercourse for three or four days after menstruation.

But notice — and this is one of the main criticisms of Hempel's model that I want to make — how this deflects attention from the actual concern of social scientists. The Hempelian model focuses attention on the law, (d) in the example, because the whole emphasis of that model is to subsume particular events under general laws. But in this example it is not the law that commands the investigator's attention. That a rational woman who doesn't want to conceive will avoid doing what she believes brings on pregnancy is neither very profound nor interesting. In fact, it is trivial (see Louch, 1966, pp. 3–4). This issue which in fact stimulates the investigator's interest in this example is not (d) but (b): just *why* does Tiare think that conception is likely to occur during the first few days after menstruation?[9]

Of course, the Hempelian advocate could claim to be able to put the explanation for *that* in his scientific form as well. He would set down as conditions Tiare's beliefs that conception results from the mingling of semen and womb-blood, and that the uterus is a mechanical organ which is open only during and immediately after menstruation. Then he would formulate a law that any rational person holding those beliefs would further believe that conception is likely to occur during the first few days following menstruation. Therefore, comes the triumphant conclusion, Tiare invariably (or with high probability) believes it. But again, the Hempelian model throws the inquiry out of focus. Now the issue of concern is not that Tiare in fact affirms a belief that is the logical implication of some other beliefs she holds. That goes without saying. The question is rather, why does she hold

those other beliefs about the nature of conception and the mechanics
of the uterus?

My argument is not that explanations which give people's reasons
for acting or which outline the logic of their beliefs and other institutions cannot be crammed into Hempel's nomological model. As we
have just seen, they can. But to do so badly muddles our understanding of how the investigation actually proceeds. At each new step in
the inquiry it requires that we stop, frame a 'law' which in fact is taken
for granted or trivial, and it falsely implies that the use of that
'law' is actually the fulcrum of the whole investigation. My point
here is really the same as that made about Hempel in the main text
of this chapter. His model is in fact useful for the confirmation of
theories. (If we wanted to confirm a hypothesis about Tiare's beliefs
or unarticulated presuppositions underpinning her beliefs, our
deduction of an empirically testable implication of the hypothesis
would fit easily in Hempel's model.) But that model does not cover
the entire process of investigation. Especially does it involve distortion of theory formation, the development of explanation and understanding. As our examples have shown, attempting to force that part
of investigation into the Hempelian mold results in throwing the
object of inquiry completely out of focus.

To this point we have been concerned with Hempel's covering-law
model as a whole and its relation to various phases of scientific
investigation. Now I would like to turn specifically to the laws
around which Hempel's approved explanations revolve, in order to
offer a suggestion for why such explanations seem so often to focus
on trivia. A scientific law is a *general* proposition, and the kinds of
'laws' we came up with in the foregoing examples scarcely fit that
criterion. A full rendition of the 'law' in one of them, for example,
would read: 'Any rational woman who does not want to get pregnant
and who believes that pregnancy is likely to result from sexual
intercourse during the first three or four days after menstruation will
avoid intercourse during those days.' This is scarcely a general
proposition about human behavior. It is so specific that it hardly
qualifies as a 'law' at all, but should perhaps be termed a 'singular
hypothetical' instead (see Dray, 1967).

The Hempelian might retort that such propositions can be expanded to a satisfactory degree of generality — but that is a hazardous
operation which can deal the *coup de grace* to these 'laws.' For
example, one might generalize the 'law' just stated as follows: any

rational woman who does not want to get pregnant will avoid sexual intercourse during the time she thinks conception is likely to occur. Still, the whole issue of conception may be too specific, so we might generalize further: any rational person who wants to avoid a given occurrence will avoid doing what that person thinks is likely to bring about that occurrence. But why stop there? More intermediate steps in the generalizing process could be specified, but its inevitable end is: any rational person acts in accordance with his ideas and beliefs. Now that is clearly not a law at all, but a tautology, or a *definition* of a rational person (see Dray, 1964, p. 14).[10] Hence we understand why the 'laws' which Hempel's model requires seem so trivial and are so often taken for granted. It is because they are not laws at all, but simply masked tautologies or definitions.

Hempel and functional analysis

One other point where Hempel's writings pass close to the concerns of this book is in his essay on 'The Logic of Functional Analysis' (1965, pp. 297–330). That essay is relevant to our interest in institutional questions for, as Hempel sees it, functionalism focuses on the articulation of elements in systems; and that includes institutions in social and cultural systems. One point of divergence is that Hempel discusses functionalism in a comparative vein whereas institutional analysis as presented here is concerned mainly with the organization of individual systems. Nevertheless, the discussion of functionalism is about as close as Hempel gets to institutional analysis, so a consideration and critique of his essay is not out of place here.

   Functionalism does not fare well in Hempel's hands. As he understands it, functional analysis aims to demonstrate that the elements which make up a system — biological, psychological, social — are necessary for that system's remaining in proper working order. Hempel's core criticism is that functional analysis fails to explain why, for any element under study, *that particular* element is necessary to the maintenance of the system. Indeed, functional analyses not infrequently imply that any of several elements — 'functional equivalents' — would serve. Anthropologists have argued, for example, that relationships in which the potential for tension and conflict exists — such as between brothers-in-law — are often hedged with norms demanding mutual restraint or even avoidance. But they have also demonstrated that, in other cultures, such potentially difficult relationships are marked by norms calling for joking and pranks.

For Hempel, this is the fatal flaw of functionalism: 'the information typically provided by a functional analysis of an item *i* affords neither deductively nor inductively adequate grounds for expecting *i* rather than one of its alternatives' (Hempel, 1965, p. 313). That is, the occurrence of the cultural element in question is not really explained, because there is no accounting for why that element occurred rather than one of its functional equivalents. One damaging consequence of this explanatory weakness is that functional analysis has little predictive power. Given a particular social situation, such as a relationship susceptible to conflict, functional analysis generates no confident prediction of one institution (a norm calling for avoidance) rather than a functional equivalent (compulsory joking, something else). These weaknesses so tarnish functional analysis in Hempel's eyes that he can see little scientific use for it beyond the study of the conditions under which a self-regulating system, when disturbed, will return to its former state.

One way to avoid the problem of functional equivalents is to define the system so narrowly that if any of its elements were different it would not be the same system. Hence, one could claim that brother-in-law avoidance is necessary to the maintenance of the system *s*, and to the question of whether compulsory joking would not work as well one would answer no, that is necessary to the maintenance of the quite different system *s'*. Asked about the difference between *s* and *s'*, one replies that in the one brothers-in-law avoid each other and in the other they joke together.

Clearly this procedure will not do. Hempel quite properly labels it 'unilluminating' and points out that 'consistent use of this type of argument would safeguard the postulate of the functional indispensability of every cultural item against any conceivable empirical disconfirmation — but at the cost of turning it from an empirical hypothesis into a covert definitional truth' (1965, p. 312).[11] But while he is unquestionably correct in this point, it is precisely from here that we can go on to demonstrate that Hempel's critique of functional analysis based on the problem of functional equivalence is illogical and unacceptable.

First of all, it is clear that when Hempel speaks of a 'system' he means not a single, empirical system but a *class* of such empirical systems. Moreover, there must be room for at least some differences among the empirical systems which compose the class. If this were not the case, then Hempel would be committed to the unilluminating argument that any change in any element of a system entails the termination of that system and the establishment of a new one. As we have seen, Hempel explicitly and properly rejects that argument.

The empirical systems which form a class are composed of elements. Those elements must be similar, or else the systems they compose would not form a class. But the elements of the different systems cannot be identical, because in that case there would be no differences among the systems which form the class. Hence, when we speak of a class of systems made up of certain elements, by 'elements' we mean not empirical elements but *classes* of empirical elements. Moreover, there must be room for variation among the empirical elements which form a class. As already established, this is necessary if there can be differences among the empirical systems which form the class. This is my main point: if by 'system' we mean a class of empirical systems among which there are differences, then by any 'element' which belongs to that system we necessarily must mean a class of empirical elements among which there are also differences.

Now we are in a position to see clearly the logical flaw in Hempel's treatment of functional analysis. In the formula, item or element i is necessary to the maintenance of system s, Hempel takes s to be a class of empirical systems among which there are differences, and then he faults functional analysis for its inability to explain why some particular, empirical element i occurs rather than a functional equivalent. But here Hempel commits an error in logic — a category mistake, a mixing of levels of generalization. As we have established, if s is taken as a class of systems, then i must be taken as a *class* of elements also, not as a single, empirical element. The 'functional equivalents' Hempel speaks of are in fact empirical members of such a class of elements. The inability to distinguish between functional equivalents is no flaw in functional analysis; it is built into its logic. When we talk about a class of systems, we can only talk about a class of elements (functional equivalents) at a corresponding level of generalization. There can be no further specification of the elements without narrower definition of the class of systems. Hempel's failure to recognize this is the fallacy in his critique of functionalism.

The definition of a class of systems can in fact be broadened or narrowed, and the specificity of explanation and prediction provided by functional analysis varies accordingly. For example, if we

are talking about the class of systems in which there is potential
conflict between brothers-in-law, we might predict that norms ordain-
ing joking, avoidance, or restraint between brothers-in-law will
invariably or with high probability be present. But if the class of
systems is narrowed, say to systems in which there is potential conflict
between brothers-in-law *and* in which the relation between brothers
and sisters is hedged with restraint or avoidance, then we might
predict that norms enjoining restraint or avoidance (but not joking)
between brothers-in-law will invariably or with high probability
be present.[12] Further circumscribing the class of systems would allow
for the generation of hypotheses specifying norms of restraint only,
or avoidance only, between brothers-in-law. The process of narrower
specification of classes of systems can of course be pursued to the
final (and unilluminating) point of saying that for any single, empirical
system to be maintained in the single, empirical form and functioning
it has, it is necessary for each of the empirical elements which compose
that system to be present and unaltered.

Let me close by repeating that the functional analysis just discussed
is not the same as the institutional analysis which is the main subject
of this book. As I have already pointed out, functional analysis as
Hempel sees it and as I have discussed it is basically a comparative
enterprise, whereas institutional analysis as presented here is concerned primarily with working out the logic of individual systems.
Again, all the talk about the necessary presence of certain elements if
systems are to be maintained tends to attribute to functionalism a
teleological cast, the implicit axiom that each human culture or
social system is a perfectly integrated mechanism, and an unwilling-
ness to recognize sociocultural change coupled with an inability to
deal with it. I personally doubt that any of these characteristics are
necessary implications of functional analysis, but to establish that
point would require detailed exploration of the logic of functionalism
which I cannot attempt here. Let me just state that while institutional
analysis seeks the logic of cultures, it does not cast it in teleological
terms, there is no anticipation that such a logic will be perfectly
harmonious (institutions can clash as well as mesh), and there is
nothing in it which makes it unsuited to deal with change. Quite the
contrary, it provides an ideal lens for looking at history as the pat-
terned development of systems of institutions, Hence, I would hold
that institutional analysis, as I understand it, is not susceptible to the
teleological, atemporal, and other charges that have been raised

against functionalism. Despite its differences from institutional analysis I have pursued this discussion of functionalism because, given his high standing among scientists and philosophers, Hempel's ill-aimed critique of functional analysis may have struck it a rather more severe blow than it deserves, and I think it is time for a reappraisal.

Chapter 5

Some anthropological applications

The purpose of the foregoing chapters has been to contribute to the clarification of some of the basic issues which confront the idea of social science. In this concluding chapter I will briefly indicate the utility of the concepts discussed here by applying them to a few current issues in my own discipline of anthropology.

Unrecognized symbols

The analysis of symbols, as in the work of Mary Douglas (1966, 1970) and Victor Turner (1967, 1973), is an important part of anthropology today. I want to discuss just one — quite basic — question connected with it: can we legitimately say that symbols have meanings of which the natives are unaware?

Imagine, for example, that one wants to study the symbolism associated with water in the Judeo-Christian religious tradition. Certainly it symbolizes cleansing of sin, as in its use in baptism to wash away original sin and Pilate's attempt to wash his hands of Christ's death. And God used water to cleanse the world of sinners in the Old Testament flood. Holy water is used upon entering a Catholic church, again symbolizing cleansing and perhaps even rebaptism. Both here and in baptism, the water is used together with the sign of the cross. This relates to the crucifixion, which also is significant for the cleansing or forgiveness of sins. There is particularly a symbolic association between water and blood, for it is often said that we are washed with Christ's blood. And a central element in the Eucharist, a rite concerned with the forgiveness or washing away of sin, is wine — symbolizing Christ's blood. One might further link the association of blood and water to the statement that, when Christ's side was pierced, there flowed out blood and water. Fire and the Holy Spirit are also associated symbolically with water as cleansing agents, for John the Baptist said that whereas he baptized with water, the one who came after him would baptize with fire and the Holy Spirit. And because the Holy Spirit came at Pentecost in the gift of tongues, one might add the Christian message or *words* in their creative and redeeming power to the list of symbolic cleansing agents. Furthermore one might detect a symbolic use of water in distinguishing the righteous or favored of God from sinners, in that the latter are susceptible to its destructive power (the flood drowned all sinners, the Red Sea swallowed up the Egyptian army) while the former are not (Noah floated on the water in his ark and Moses in his cradle, the sea divided for the Israelites, Jesus walked on the water).

Certainly many of the meanings and associations specified in such an analysis of the symbolism of water would not be offered by ordinary laymen; by the time it was done the analysis would doubtless include points not present in the exegesis of theologians. (This is not to say that the theologians or laymen could not understand such symbolic associations once they were pointed out; nor does it prejudge whether or not they will accept them as valid.) To reiterate the question, is this analytic procedure legitimate? Are we justified in saying that symbols have certain meanings when no native is aware of them?

Arguments have been entered on both sides of this question. Turner does not limit analysis to native exegesis. When he analyzes the 'operational' and 'positional' meaning of symbols (how symbols are used and how they relate to other symbols), he claims to find meaning in Ndembu symbols of which no native is aware (Turner, 1967, pp. 284–5). Others, anxious to avoid reading meanings into symbols which are not there, proceed more cautiously. Monica Wilson carefully limited her study of Nyakyusa rituals to native interpretations (1957, p. 6). And Nadel's incisive reasoning is that once we step beyond native awareness we can no longer be said to be dealing with symbols at all: 'In my view uncomprehended symbols have no part in social enquiry; their social effectiveness lies in their capacity to indicate, and if they indicate nothing to the actors, they are, from our point of view, irrelevant and indeed no longer symbols (whatever their significance for the psychologist or psycho-analyst)' (Nadel, 1954, p. 108). To be sure, the symbols may suggest further meanings to an anthropologist like Turner, but presumably the object of study is Ndembu symbolism, not Turner symbolism.

My own position on this issue is entirely on the side of Turner and, as will become clear in a moment, for reasons very like his. But first, because Nadel's argument to the contrary seems logically compelling, let me begin by examining what he said. Nadel argues that the only socially effective meanings a symbol can have must be located in native minds. These meanings may be recognized consciously or lurk in the subconscious, but if they are not in native minds they cannot exist. From this beginning it is perfectly logical to conclude, as Nadel does, that a symbol symbolizes what the actors think it does, and nothing more. But that is like saying that a language has no grammatical rules other than those which native speakers can formulate. I would argue instead that, just as a grammatical rule is a statement of a regularity perceived in the use of language, so we can make statements about the meaning of symbols, statements which are formulations of regularities in the use of those symbols. Meaning in this sense is of the variety I have labeled 'implicational'; it concerns the logical structure of and relations among the institutions which compose the culture. With their fertile capacity for marking associations among concepts, beliefs, values, customs and other institutions, symbols are an integral part of the implicational meaning of any culture. And that is so whether or not the natives happen to be aware of the full implicational meaning of any symbol, because that meaning has its source in the organization of institutions, not in the minds of men. We are of course deeply interested in anything natives say about the meaning of their symbols, but we are not limited to that because our prime source of information on the implicational meaning of symbols is patterns of their use. Hence the argument of this book supports entirely the proposition that the analysis of symbols need not cease at the outer boundaries of native exegesis.

Returning now to Turner, while his position on the meaning of symbols is complicated and involves a number of considerations not touched upon here (see especially 1967, pp. 19–47), I think the argument I have just offered finds important precedent in what he said. This is particularly so in the following passage, where Turner urges a broad contextual analysis of the social use of symbols (1967, pp. 46–7).

> Here the significant elements of a symbol's meaning are related to what it does and what is done to it by and for whom. These aspects can only be understood if one takes into account from the beginning, and represents by appropriate theoretical constructs, the total field situation in which the symbol occurs. This situation would include the structure of the group that performs the ritual we observe, its basic organizing principles and perdurable relationships, and, in addition, its extant division into transient alliances and factions on the basis of immediate interest and ambitions, for both abiding structure and recurrent forms of conflict and selfish interest are stereotyped in ritual symbolism.

Translated into the terminology of this book, it seems to me that in this passage Turner urges that symbols be subjected to institutional analysis in order to determine their implicational meaning.

Culture and behavior

David Schneider is one anthropologist who has recently advocated an approach to culture which sounds very much like the institutional analysis discussed in this book: 'The problem I have posed is that of describing and treating culture as an independent system and of analyzing it in its own terms; that is, as a coherent system of symbols and meanings' (Schneider, 1968, p. 8). Similar as this may seem to institutional analysis, closer scrutiny reveals a number of important differences. Hence in addition to what can be learned from it in its own right, an examination of Schneider's approach can help further clarify, by contrast, what is meant by institutional analysis.

One of the fundamental questions before modern anthropology is whether, in studying culture, we should study the statistical regularities of the choices people make and the ways they actually behave, or the norms, values, and criteria which in some sense lie 'behind' actual behavior.[1] Schneider does not equivocate on this point: when we study culture we are concerned with the conventional definitions, symbols and meanings whereby people construe reality, the values, norms and rules which shape their notion of proper behavior. Culture is not to be confused with actual behavior, nor even with patterns of actual behavior (Schneider, 1968, p. 5).[2] Indeed, so sharply does Schneider draw the line between culture and behavior that 'these two are to be understood as *independent* of each other and not as being in tautologous relationship. That is, the definition of the (cultural) units and rules is *not* based on, defined by, drawn from, constructed in accord with, or developed in terms of the observations of behavior in any direct, simple sense' (1968, p. 6, Schneider's italics).

At the same time, we are assured that such difference and independence do not remove culture entirely from the realm of actual behavior: 'Culture *is* actual, observable behavior, but of only one specially restricted kind' (1968, p. 5, Schneider's italics; see also Silverman, 1971, pp. 8–9). Schneider's sequel makes it clear that the kind of behavior which is culture consists of people's definitions of their conventional concepts, beliefs, values, symbols, rules and norms. For example, the distinction between a regularity of actual behavior (which is not culture) and the expression of a rule of definition (which is culture) seems to be the point of a passage like this one: 'The regularity "people actually stop for red lights" is different in a fundamental and important way from the regularity "people are by law supposed to stop for red lights" ' (Schneider, 1968, p. 6).

I think Schneider's view of culture is most intelligible if we recognize that, although definitions, ideas, symbols, constructs of all sorts are included among cultural things, it is oriented primarily toward norms. Everyone knows that people may specify a norm or rule for proper behavior in particular circumstances when in fact not everyone (perhaps hardly anyone) in those circumstances actually follows the rule and yet such noncompliance does not deter people from continuing to specify the rule. Schneider's sharp distinction between culture (in this case, the rule) and actual behavior (the degree of actual compliance with the rule) seems particularly adapted to this kind of situation, which one encounters far more frequently with norms than with symbols and other constructs.

Perhaps his is an effective way of dealing with discrepancies between what people say should be done and what they actually do (more of that below). Nevertheless, I cannot accept Schneider's radical separation of culture from actual behavior, because I think it raises more serious problems than it lays to rest. Foremost among the problems occasioned by Schneider's theory is the connection between culture and behavior: if these are to be so sharply distinguished, precisely what relation obtains between them? There are moments when Schneider seems to think that they are not related at all. We have already quoted his assertion that culture and behavior are independent. Moreover, he contends that the evidence of actual behavior — even when that evidence is 100 per cent contrary to the cultural rule — 'is quite irrelevant to the question of whether there is or is not a cultural unit, a cultural concept, a cultural rule, a cultural entity' (1968, p. 7). But this expands ultimately to the proposition that a society may properly be said to have a certain culture although none of the members of that society ever conforms to any of its norms or rules or acts in accordance with any of its symbols or definitions. The image evoked is of culture floating freely over the busy hive of actual behavior, neither influencing nor being affected by what goes on here. It is a notion which I think most would reject as absurd.

Nor do I think Schneider would affirm it, for at other moments he does recognize relations of some sort between culture and behavior. He admits, for example, that observation of actual behavior can yield hypotheses — if no more than hypotheses — about cultural constructs (1968, p. 7). And he acknowledges that one legitimate and essential problem (if not the one he has chosen) 'is to chart the relationship between the actual states of affairs and the cultural constructs so that we can discover how the cultural constructs are generated, the laws governing their change, and in just what ways they are systematically related to the actual state of affairs of life' (1968, p. 7). Since Schneider clearly does perceive that culture and behavior are related, we are anxious to know in precisely what way. But in this we are disappointed because, that not being the problem treated in his book, he does not say.

While I am in complete sympathy with Schneider's aim to study culture in its own terms, I do not think his distinction between culture and behavior is a useful one. Very much like Cartesian dualism, that distinction divides reality into two parts and then fails to provide a coherent and satisfying account of the relations between them. This brings us to the crux of the difference between Schneider's approach and institutional analysis as defined in this book. For Schneider the critical distinction is concrete. It is really out there in the data we

MIC—H

study: 'culture' is one particular kind of observable behavior (definitions of roles, norms, values, symbols), while 'behavior' is the rest of
observable behavior (Schneider, 1968, pp. 5–6). For institutional
analysis as I construe it, the analogous distinction (analogous, not
coterminous) — between individual and institutional questions —
is analytic. It is not found in the data themselves, but in the ways we
look at the data.[3]

It is not, as Schneider would have it, that culture is one quite
restricted kind of human activity while all the rest of behavior is
something else. We should study culture *in* behavior, not in spite of it.
With the possible exception of certain purely physiological processes
like breathing and digestion, culture is involved in everything people
do. Therefore, to study culture in its own terms is precisely to
study the full range of actual behavior — but from a particular point
of view. That point of view is defined by what I have termed institutional questions: questions about the beliefs, norms, symbols, kinds
of social relationships and other institutions which are expressed in
actual behavior, and about the structure or logical relations among
such institutions. Be very clear about this: whereas Schneider says
that such 'cultural units' *are* actual behavior of one special kind, I
hold that they are *expressed in* (and hence analytically abstracted
from) actual behavior of all kinds. Cultural definitions, symbols,
rules are embedded not only in pronouncements about kinship
terminology, right belief or proper manners, but also in handshakes,
in pedestrian paths around rather than under ladders, in an arched
eyebrow when someone is observed using the wrong fork, even in the
running of a red light — which, after all, would be considered a very
different kind of act by both the agent and the analyst were there no
law against it.

Earlier I noted that Schneider's distinction between culture and
actual behavior seems particularly adapted to cases where people
do not follow expressed laws, rules or norms. Let me now return to
that point with the contention that institutional analysis, which
does not make Schneider's distinction, in fact provides a more
accurate construal of such situations. If the culturally proper thing
to do were always clear and unequivocal, with no norms or values
supporting the discrepant actual event (as is often — but by no means
always — the case with running red lights), then Schneider's view of
the matter would be quite satisfactory. The rule or behavior expecta-
tion is culture; the actual behavior is something else. But life is

seldom so simple. In many situations (such as deciding whether to tell the truth if it will hurt someone's feelings, or deciding whether to expose your children to the teachings of religion if you have rejected them) cultural norms and values can be found on both sides of the question, as can idiosyncratic motives, reasons, or desires. Here it is not possible to explain the discrepancy between certain norms and what was actually done by saying that the norms are culture and the act is not — for there are other norms, just as 'cultural' as the first, to which the act conforms. Hence, I would argue that the utility of Schneider's model for accounting for discrepancies between expressed norms and actual behavior is really quite limited. In fact, the model may even be misleading in that it could incline one to an oversimplified and hence distorted view of many human situations. I would hold that institutional analysis, which does not condition one to dismiss actual behavior as something other than culture, provides the better model for accurate understanding.

Ecological anthropology

An ecological perspective is increasingly popular in contemporary American anthropology. It is particularly relevant to this book, because it entails an extension of the basic view of social science adopted here. My discussion will focus on ecological anthropology as articulated by Roy Rappaport. According to Rappaport (1971, p. 243, his italics):

> The ecological perspective leads us to ask whether behavior undertaken with respect to social, economic, political, or religious conventions contributes to or threatens the survival and well-being of the actors, and whether this behavior maintains or degrades the ecological systems in which it occurs. *While the questions are asked about cultural phenomena, they are answered in terms of the effects of culturally informed behavior on biological systems: organisms, populations and eco-systems.*

Rappaport explains that this perspective requires the recognition of two distinct models for what people do. The 'cognized model' refers to the people's own view of their situation, and they act in terms of that model. The 'operational model' refers to the outside analyst's view of the ecological system of which the people and their culture are parts (Rappaport, 1971, p. 247). The ecological anthropologist is especially concerned with the relation between these two models; specifically, with 'the effects of behavior undertaken with respect to the cognized model on the ecosystem as it is represented in the operational model. In this way it becomes possible to assess the adaptiveness not only of overt human behavior, but even of the ideology which informs that behavior' (Rappaport, 1971, p. 248). In other words, people's actions and their cultural beliefs, rules, institutions of all sorts are understood and evaluated according to their adaptiveness in the ecosystem, as this is perceived by the anthropologist.

Pig festivals of the Maring of New Guinea provide Rappaport with his favorite example of ecological analysis (1967, 1968, 1971). Maring groups sacrifice large number of pigs at various intervals over a period of several years following a war. Most of the group's pigs are sacrificed, sparing only the juveniles to replenish the herd. At such times there is much feasting on pork, for Maring hold that the spirits to whom the pigs are sacrificed consume their spirits, while living men consume the flesh.

The 'cognized model' or native view of these rites is that the spirits helped the group in the recent war, and the pig sacrifices are their repayment. No military effort could be successful without the aid of the spirits, and these are not over-indulgent creditors. Hence the Maring undertake no new war until the debts to the spirits for the last one are fully discharged, a process which may take ten or more years.

Rappaport has constructed his own 'operational model' for Maring pig sacrifices, viewing them from the perspective of ecological anthropology. This model focuses on the effects of the size and density of the pig population on the ecosystem. When the pig population approaches a certain level, a number of ecologically non-adaptive conditions emerge. One is that more gardens must be planted in order to provide enough food for the pigs. Women tend gardens, and when pigs are numerous their gardening work is significantly augmented, which diminishes women's time and energy for other tasks and increases their complaints. Another effect of numerous pigs is that they are more likely to root up gardens, resulting in increased friction between neighbors when the pigs of one break into the garden of the other. The periodic large-scale sacrifices of pigs act, in the operational model, as an ecological thermostat which counteracts such nonadaptive conditions and maintains the pig population within certain parameters. Because it takes a number of years for the pig population to attain the level adequate for sacrifices, and because Maring do not go to battle before pig sacrifices have fully paid the spirits for their assistance in the previous war, Rappaport holds that the pig rituals also serve to limit the frequency of warfare among the Maring.

As is clear from the foregoing example, the ecological anthropologist is not concerned primarily with the cognized model as a thing in itself. Instead, he is interested in it as one of several elements in his operational model of the total ecosystem. He is even prepared to *evaluate* the cognized model according to its 'functional and adaptive effectiveness' in the ecosystem, as represented in his operational model (Rappaport, 1971, pp. 247–8). Given my emphasis on understanding other cultures in their own terms, according to their intrinsic meaning, this expressed readiness to apprehend and evaluate a 'cognized model' by criteria utterly alien to it led me to adopt a very negative attitude toward ecological anthropology — until quite recently. In fact, I used Rappaport's analysis of Maring pig festivals in many seminars and lectures as my favorite example of how *not* to go about understanding an alien culture. But I have changed my mind. I of course still hold that culture is intrinsically meaningful and should therefore be understood internally; this book is devoted to establishing, elaborating, and clarifying those very points. However, I now think that Rappaport's mode of investigation is entirely legitimate. I even think that it exemplifies an important expansion of the general approach this book takes to social science, including its stress on internal understanding.

When we talk about internal understanding, the critical question becomes, 'internal *to what*?' The understanding which comes from institutional analysis is internal to the culture — involving as it does the intrinsic, implicational meaning of institutions which make up that culture. But it is not necessarily internal to the *people* who carry and perpetuate that culture, for they may be unaware of much of its meaning. I consider this one of the main advantages of the distinction between individual and institutional questions: it enables us to talk about internal understanding of other cultures even when we have gone beyond the awareness of natives. This is because when one asks institutional questions the focus of inquiry is not people at all, but on culture — institutions and their organization. In precisely the same way, I now think that Rappaport's ecological approach does indeed provide internal understanding. It is internal, however, neither to the people under study nor to their culture. Instead, it is internal to the *ecosystem*. When regular relations are detected between sexual division of labor and daily work patterns, amount of land under cultivation, frequency of warfare, ideology and ritual, and size and density of pig populations, that is a demonstration of some of the ways in which the ecosystem *is* a system. In a word, it lays bare the dynamic structure or organization of the ecosystem — and that, in my lexicon, constitutes internal understanding of it.

Ecological anthropology expands the point of view about social science adapted in this book by its implication that the distinction between individual and institutional questions is not exhaustive. A third category should be added: ecological questions. Individual questions concern people's intentions, reasons, motivations, drives and hence lead to internal understanding of people. Institutional questions concern beliefs, definitions, norms, customs, patterns of behavior and their organization and thus provide internal understanding of culture. Analogously, ecological questions concern climate, geomorphology, flora, fauna, and their interrelations, and thus provide internal understanding of the ecosystem. When one asks specifically *anthropological* ecological questions the focus is on the ways in which human beings — with their biological and psychological make up and their cultural institutions — participate in the ecosystem.

Let me stress again here, as I did in Chapter 1, that these distinctions are between *kinds of questions* or *analytic points of view*. We are emphatically *not* dealing with three levels of empirical reality (psychological, cultural, ecological), nor with three levels of analysis in the sense that they are on different planes of abstraction. Individual, institutional, and anthropological ecological questions all refer to the same chunk of empirical reality — human action. They differ not in that one kind of question is reducible to another, but because they represent different perspectives on the reality of human action. They ask about human action in relation to different things: the minds of the people engaging in the action, the cultural institutions that action represents, and the ecosystem in which that action participates.[4]

Sorting out the kinds of questions asked can occasionally demonstrate that academic disagreements are more apparent than real. For example, Marshall Sahlins and Irving Goldman offer apparently rival explanations for cultural variation in Polynesia. For Sahlins (1957, 1958) it is essentially a matter of adaptation to environmental conditions such as high islands *v.* atolls and spatial concentration *v.* dispersal of resources. By contrast, Goldman (1955, 1958, 1960, 1970) accounts for the same thing by placing Polynesian societies at different stages of an evolutionary progression defined by the internal dynamics of the Polynesian system of stratification and status rivalry among those of high rank. But these explanations need not be seen as conflicting, because Sahlins is asking ecological questions whereas Goldman asks institutional questions. This is not to say that their analyses are both right or satisfactory. (In fact, I think there are problems with each.) However, I do maintain that Sahlins's and Goldman's interpretations are not squarely opposed because, although they deal with the same data, they do so from different analytic perspectives.

Notes

1 The subject matter of social science

1 My ideas here are very close to Popper's in his lucid discussions (1968, 1969) of the difference between subjective and objective thought (see also Jarvie, 1972, Chapter 6).

2 The passage quoted is from some introductory remarks by H. P. Rickman, editor of the Dilthey volume.

3 To be sure, a few institutions like the American form of government were explicitly designed and can hence legitimately be treated in terms of their intentional meaning, although a good share of any such discussion would be devoted to how such institutions have developed in unforeseen ways. But the concept of intentional meaning seems entirely alien to the vast majority of customs and institutions — the British constitution, capitalism, marriage, motherhood, honor, patrilineal descent, preferential cross-cousin marriage, Oxford University — because no one ever sat down and designed them.

4 See also Langer (1957, pp. 53-6), Rickman (1967, p. 95) and L. White (1969, p. xxv).

5 See also Winch (1958, p. 108). Since dissatisfaction with some of Dilthey's formulations led us to the discussion of implicational meaning, it should be noted that he also recognized meaning in the part–whole relationship (Tuttle, 1969, pp. 15–16, 80–7).

6 It may seem curious to look to Collingwood for guidance in the study of institutional questions, because he has been criticized by both Hodges (1944, p. 103) and Popper (1968, p. 29) for reducing socio-cultural phenomena to psychological ones. Such a criticism may apply to Collingwood's stress on the re-enactment of the thought of past

individuals for historical understanding (1946), but as the sequel will demonstrate it is far from the mark with regard to his concept of metaphysics.

7 I believe this 'question-and-answer complex' is what Collingwood elsewhere termed 'reflective thought' (1946, pp. 307–15). It is simply a series of logical implications.

8 Readers who wish to explore Collingwood's logic of question and answer and the concept of absolute presuppositions further might begin with a criticism by Donagan (1962, pp. 66–93) and a defense by Rynin (1964). See also the further remarks to this chapter.

9 In talking about the dynamics of cultural implications I am very close to Popper's concept of unintended consequences (see Popper, 1963, pp. 96–7).

10 Needham (1962) has taken pains to see that this and other short-comings in Homans's and Schneider's book do not go unnoticed.

11 While we may currently lack the technology to verify the second proposition in fact, we can easily specify a verification procedure: take a spaceship to Mars and look.

12 These examples of meaningless propositions are derived from Waismann (1965, pp. 38, 326–8).

13 I am indebted for this intriguing group of words to my brother, Dr Ervin Hanson.

14 Logical positivists differ among themselves on this point. For example, Schlick grants meaning to sentences about the afterlife or disembodied souls, whereas Ayer does not (Aldrich, 1949).

15 On the following page Collingwood makes it clear that the beliefs or presuppositions in question here are absolute presuppositions.

16 As already noted, Collingwood had much less to say about meaning than truth. My interpretation is based on the fact that he speaks of truth and meaning together, such as 'whether a given proposition is true or false, significant or meaningless, depends on what question it was meant to answer' (1939, p. 39). It should be mentioned that in another work (1940, pp. 162–71), while nothing explicit is said, he does seem to reason from the implicit premise that absolute presuppositions are meaningful.

17 In this discussion I do not claim to set down what truth and meaning 'really' or absolutely are. I have argued that there are no such things as absolute truth or absolute meaning. I am talking about those concepts in our own culture — Western civilization — especially in its scholarly precincts. There is always a reflexive quality to such discussions: what we say about other cultures and systems of thought is applicable also to our own. Eventually this raises certain problems regarding cross-cultural understanding, which will be discussed in Chapter 3.

18 One might interpret Collingwood himself as involving implications in his concept of truth, although he is far from clear on these matters. One of his criteria for a true proposition is that it be the 'right' answer to its question (1939, p. 38), and he holds that a 'right' answer is one which 'enables us to get ahead with the process of questioning and

answering' (1939, p. 37). I take it, then, that a 'right' answer is one which has *implications*. Caution is necessary here, however, because he also holds that a 'right' answer can be false, as happens if it is part of a *reductio ad absurdum* (1939, pp. 37–8). But then one wonders again what makes a proposition true for Collingwood, especially when it is noticed that his concept may involve circularity because the first criterion of a 'true' proposition is that it 'belongs to a question-and-answer complex which as a whole is "true" in the proper sense of the word' (1939, p. 38). What, then, makes a question-and-answer complex true?

19 A more detailed discussion of meaning and truth would make more distinctions between those concepts than is done here. For example, meaning seems to be logically prior to truth in that the question of whether a sentence is true or false comes up only if the sentence is meaningful. That question does not arise for meaningless or nonsensical sentences. Such refinements, however, would not affect the conclusion reached here.

2   Judging other cultures

1 This might sound preposterous, but consider the question now frequently faced by members of our own society: does one show love for parents in the final stages of cancer by prolonging their lives and suffering via drugs and other artificial means, or by letting them die?

2 *American Anthropologist*, vol. 49, pp. 539–43, 1947.

3 MacIntyre (1964) seems to blur this distinction, as Alston (1964) points out. Leoni, on the other hand, sees it clearly (Leoni, 1961).

4 See Bruner and Spindler (1963, p. 142), Tennekes (1971, p. 9), and the 'Statement on Human Rights' (*American Anthropologist*, vol. 49, pp. 539–43, 1947), submitted by the Executive Committee of the American Anthropological Association to the United Nations Commission on Human Rights.

5 The contrast in attitudes between Vivas and most anthropologists is fascinating. For example, when Vivas judges relativism to be 'pernicious' because its 'effect is to bruise, if not to destroy, the moral fibre of students' (1961, p. 61), he is probably referring to the sort of thing which anthropologists prefer to cast in terms such as: 'Combatting ethnocentrism or provincialism has been named frequently as one of the main objectives of teaching anthropology,' or 'relativism has been found useful for showing students their place in the pattern of their own culture . . . or the place of Western culture as one among many' (Albert, 1963, pp. 561, 563).

6 This arouses curiosity as to the status of Western scholarship in the humanities (history, philosophy, even philosophy of science) compared with other cultures.

7 See also MacIntyre, 1967.

8 Schmidt (1955, pp. 790–1) distinguishes between the thesis and method of cultural relativism, Obeyesekere (1966) between philosophical and

methodological relativism. Substantially the same distinction is made in all cases.

3 Understanding other cultures

1 Foreign institutions may be the source of hints or leads in the process of investigation, but they should not provide the standards against which the institution in question is measured and known. Cross-cultural comparison is possible — for example, Navajo witchcraft and Zande witchcraft may have more in common than either has with Western science — but only *after* each institution has been understood in the context of its own culture.

2 But see also Winch (1964), where he refines his argument with special reference to anthropology.

3 See B. Wilson (1970) for a compilation of many of the important contributions to that debate.

4 I do not wish to cast a blanket indictment on Hollis for this passage. As we shall see below, in other places he is far more precise in his use of words.

5 Let me hasten to add that I do think the criterion of empirical verifiability is applicable to the doing of social science, including the analysis of alien and nonempirical systems of belief. For example, I do not think the criterion of empirical verifiability can be legitimately applied to determine the truth or accuracy of Australian aboriginal concepts of the 'Dreaming' or Christian ideas of original sin and grace, but I *do* think that criterion can and should be applied in assessing the truth or accuracy of a social scientist's description and analysis of those beliefs.

6 Consider Hollis's definition of the rationality of 'ritual beliefs': 'a ritual belief p is rational if and only if there is a belief q such that q supplies a reason for holding p and p does not entail the falsity of q.' Later on the same page, he provides the definition with a theological content: theologians 'may take religion to begin with faith and end with mystery but they also hold that every belief which can be made explicit either makes rational another belief or is made rational by another belief or both' (Hollis, 1968, p. 243). There can be no clearer statement of what I have called implicational meaning than this.

7 See F. A. Hanson (1970b) for a fuller discussion of the Rapan theory of conception.

8 This, of course, does not necessarily entail *agreeing* with them — a point argued in detail in Chapter 2.

9 There is a large and lively literature on just what is entailed by *Verstehen* or re-enactment. For some they imply an intuitive or immediate apprehension which may be deemed infallible and is at any rate impossible to verify — a concept of understanding which smacks of mysticism and may even be meaningless. Others see them as representing a straightforward means of knowing which depends on a careful sifting of evidence and is susceptible to verification or falsification by

evidence. Dilthey, Collingwood and Dray would fall under the latter category. In addition to the references already cited, see Cebik (1970), Donagan (1956), Gardiner (1952, pp. 48–9, 128; 1966), Louch (1966, pp. 2–4, 201–2) and Walsh (1967, pp. 57–8).

10 In a more recent paper (1969) Burling equivocates somewhat on this point.

11 Dilthey (Rickman, 1960, p. 315), Jarvie (1970, p. 232), and Needham (1972, pp. 243–6) made further variations on this theme.

12 Some attempts to deal with the problem of psychological validity are discussed in the further remarks to this chapter.

13 Hence our topic is closely connected to the philosophers' problem of other minds.

14 For summaries of Cartesian dualism, see Ryle (1949, pp. 11–14) and A. White (1967, pp. 31–8).

15 Runciman (1972, pp. 37–40) cogently points out that the issue here is not so much our values as our theoretical presuppositions.

16 Please note that I am not criticizing everything Weber meant by 'ideal types,' but just one usage of the term.

17 In fairness to Weber it must be noted that in a paper included in *The Methodology of the Social Sciences* he does speak of the meaning or significance of cultural phenomena (1949, p. 77). I cannot see that he works out that point very clearly, but at least his position there is that much more compatible with the approach I am advocating.
   Another example of an 'as if' approach is one of my papers (F. A. Hanson, 1970c). Today I would level the same criticism against that as I have brought here against Weber and Maquet.

18 See also Jarvie (1972, ch. 6).

19 Popper's point reads very much like Kuhn's (1962) concern for seeing scientific theories in the context of more general 'paradigms,' or like Collingwood's logic of question-and-answer in which propositions must be understood in terms of the questions they were meant to answer (1939, p. 33). See also Popper (1969, pp. 240, 270–1).

20 I could not be in more agreement with Popper that it is a serious mistake to attempt to reduce institutional questions to individual or psychological ones. However, this particular criticism may be closer to the mark regarding Collingwood than Dilthey (see Hodges, 1944, p. 103). And this criticism is apt to Collingwood, I would argue, only with respect to his concept of understanding by re-enactment. In other contexts Collingwood operated very effectively from an institutional or 'third world' perspective. In fact, as I claimed in Chapter 1, Collingwood's logic of question-and-answer strikes me as the best available model in which to cast institutional analyses.

21 Dray (1958, p. 205) acknowledges that this interpretation of Collingwood requires making choices among the papers reprinted in *The Idea of History*. The first few chapters of Collingwood's *New Leviathan* appear to support Dray's interpretation. See especially section 2.43. Louch (1966) also draws upon Ryle's concept of mind in constructing his notion of explanation in social science.

4 But is it scientific?

1 Hempel is treated only briefly at this point. Detailed discussion of some of his main ideas about social science may be found in the further remarks section of this chapter.

2 This example is taken from Hempel (1966a, p. 10). See Harré (1970, pp. 20–1) for a general critique of deductive-nomological explanation.

3 This could be refined to specify the probability of the occurrence of types A or B for any offspring.

4 See also Harré's discussion of models (1970, ch. 2) — an excellent guide to how scientists devise hypotheses.

5 The experiment would have to be run also with many other Rapans and numerous other experimental tests would have to be devised and carried out before confirmation of the theory is considered adequate. Of course, whether Te'ura would actually avoid drinking cold water on a particular day when he is hot and sweaty is a different question. As is not infrequently the case with people, on occasion he may behave inappropriately. But this involves individual as well as institutional questions, and hence would take us beyond the boundaries of institutional analysis.

6 In the terminology of this book, rational explanation would come under the category of individual questions, concerned as they are with people's intentions, motives, drives, reasons for acting.

7 This account of the Pastoral Fulani is from Stenning (1957).

8 This example is based on a more purely formal case (why did A do X?) worked out by Hempel (1965, pp. 469–72; 1966b, pp. 116–18). The account I have given is still not complete because a number of conditions are not specified — e.g. that the Pastoral Fulani own cattle, that they want them to live, that they know how to drive them north, etc. See Marquis (1973) for a model with room for most conceivable conditions.

9 Here we are near the point of Martin's valuable essay on historical explanation (1975).

10 A law is falsifiable, but if we observed a person whom we had called rational acting in opposition to his ideas and beliefs, our reaction would not be to assume our proposition about rational people had been disproven. Instead we would conclude that, in this instance at least, the person in question was not rational.

11 For his part, Hempel is willing to allow quite broad modifications within the confines of single systems. For example, he accepts an extension of 'rational technology' plus modifications in religion as a functional equivalent to magic in a primitive group (1965, pp. 311–12).

12 I do not know if this is true, but it can be taken as an empirical hypothesis with testable implications.

5 Some anthropological applications

1 Among other things, this question is at the heart of the debate among Murdock, Sahlins, Goodenough and others over the nature of cognatic or non-unilineal descent systems (see Howard, 1963, pp. 407–9; 1969, pp. 20–2).

2 Reference here is to the later Schneider (especially Schneider, 1968); an earlier Schneider (Homans and Schneider, 1955) represented a significantly different position. Schneider's distinction between culture and actual behavior has much in common with that drawn by Parsons and Shils between the cultural and social systems (1951, p. 7) — a distinction used with some elegance, incidentally, by Geertz (1957) in the analysis of a Javanese funeral.

3 The same difference of opinion crops up, among other places, in *Toward a General Theory of Action*, a volume to which both Schneider and I owe something. In the general statement of the theory the distinction between personality, social, and cultural systems smacks of the concrete in that culture is seen as referring to a different kind of *thing* from the other two (Parsons and Shils, 1951, p. 7). But in the same volume Richard Sheldon dissents (in my opinion correctly), arguing that the distinction should be entirely analytic (Parsons and Shils, 1951, pp. 39–42).

4 Doubtless these three do not exhaust the perspectives or kinds of questions that can be asked of human action. One could easily add, for example, biological questions, neurological questions, and so on.

Bibliography

ALBERT, ETHEL M. (1963), 'Value Aspects of Teaching Anthropology,' in Mandelbaum, Lasker and Albert, eds (1963), pp. 559–81.

ALDRICH, VIRGIL C. (1949), 'Messrs Schlick and Ayer on Immortality,' in Feigl and Sellars, eds (1949), pp. 171–4.

ALSTON, WILLIAM (1964), 'On Sharing Concepts,' in Hicks, ed. (1964), pp. 154–5.

ASHBY, R. W. (1956), 'Use and Verification,' *Proceedings of the Aristotelian Society*, 56, pp. 149–66.

AYER, A. J., ed. (1959), *Logical Positivism*, Chicago: Free Press.

AYER, A. J. (1970), 'An Honest Ghost?,' in Wood and Pitcher, eds (1970), pp. 53–74.

BARNES, W. H. F. (1939), 'Meaning and Verifiability,' *Philosophy*, 14, pp. 410–21.

BARRINGER, H. R., BLANKSTEN, G. I. and MACK, R. W., eds (1965), *Social Change in Developing Areas*, Cambridge, Mass.: Schenkman.

BEATTIE, J. H. M. (1970), 'On Understanding Ritual', in B. Wilson, ed. (1970), pp. 240–68.

BENEDICT, RUTH (1934), *Patterns of Culture*, Boston: Houghton Mifflin.

BERLIN, ISAIAH (1954), *Historical Inevitability*, London: Oxford University Press.

BIDNEY, DAVID (1944), 'On the Concept of Culture and Some Cultural Fallacies,' *American Anthropologist*, 46, pp. 30–44.

BIDNEY, DAVID (1950), Review of L. White (1949), in *American Anthropologist*, 52, pp. 518–19.

BORGER, ROBERT and CIOFFI, FRANK, eds (1970), *Explanation in the Behavioural Sciences*, Cambridge University Press.

BRUNER, EDWARD M. and SPINDLER, GEORGE D. (1963), 'The Introductory Course in Cultural Anthropology,' in Mandelbaum, Lasker and Albert, eds (1963), pp. 141–52.

BUNGE, MARIO (1959), *Metascientific Queries*, Springfield, Ill.: Thomas.

BURLING, ROBBINS (1964), 'Cognition and Componential Analysis: God's Truth or Hocus-Pocus?,' *American Anthropologist*, 66, pp. 20–8.

BURLING, ROBBINS (1965), 'Burmese Kinship Terminology,' in Hammel, ed. (1965), pp. 106–17.

BURLING, ROBBINS (1969), 'Linguistics and Ethnographic Description,' *American Anthropologist*, 71, pp. 817–27.

CARNAP, RUDOLF (1959), 'The Elimination of Metaphysics Through Logical Analysis of Language,' in Ayer, ed. (1959), pp. 60–81.

CASTANEDA, CARLOS (1968), *The Teachings of Don Juan*, New York: Ballantine.

CASTANEDA, CARLOS (1971), *A Separate Reality*, New York: Simon & Schuster.

CASTANEDA, CARLOS (1972), *Journey to Ixtlan*, New York: Simon & Schuster.

CEBIK, L. B. (1970), 'Collingwood: Action, Re-enactment, and Evidence,' *Philosophical Forum*, 2, pp. 68–90.

CHOMSKY, NOAM (1968a), 'Language and the Mind I,' *Columbia Forum*, 11, pp. 5–10.

CHOMSKY, NOAM (1968b), *Language and Mind*, New York: Harcourt, Brace & World.

COLLINGWOOD, R. G. (1939), *An Autobiography*, Oxford: Clarendon Press.

COLLINGWOOD, R. G. (1940), *An Essay on Metaphysics*, Oxford: Clarendon Press.

COLLINGWOOD, R. G. (1942), *The New Leviathan*, Oxford: Clarendon Press.

COLLINGWOOD, R. G. (1946), *The Idea of History*, Oxford: Clarendon Press.

COMTE, AUGUSTE (1864), *Cours de Philosophie Positive*, 2nd ed., Paris: Baillière.

DANIELSSON, BENGT (1956), *Love in the South Seas*, London: Allen & Unwin.

DANTO, ARTHUR (1966), 'The Problem of Other Periods,' *Journal of Philosophy*, 63, pp, 566–77.

DE LA CUEVA, MARIO *et al.* (1966), *Major Trends in Mexican Philosophy*, University of Notre Dame Press.

DIAMOND, STANLEY, ed. (1960), *Culture in History*, New York: Columbia University Press.

DILTHEY, WILHELM (1962), *Pattern and Meaning in History*, H. P. Rickman, ed., New York: Harper & Row.

DONAGAN, ALAN (1956), 'The Verification of Historical Theses,' *Philosophical Quarterly*, 6, pp. 193–208.

DONAGAN, ALAN (1962), *The Later Philosophy of R. G. Collingwood*, Oxford: Clarendon Press.

DOUGLAS, MARY (1966), *Purity and Danger*, London: Routledge & Kegan Paul, and New York: Praeger.

DOUGLAS, MARY (1970), *Natural Symbols*, London: Barrie & Rockliff.

DOWNS, JAMES F. (1971), *Cultures in Crisis*, New York: Glencoe Press.

DRAY, WILLIAM H. (1957a), *Laws and Explanation in History*, London: Oxford University Press.

DRAY, WILLIAM H. (1957b), 'R. G. Collingwood and the Acquaintance Theory of Knowledge,' *Revue Internationale de Philosophie*, 11, pp. 420–32.

DRAY, WILLIAM H. (1958), 'Historical Understanding as Re-Thinking,' *University of Toronto Quarterly*, 27, pp. 200–15.

DRAY, WILLIAM (1964), *Philosophy of History*, Englewood Cliffs, N.J.: Prentice-Hall.

DRAY, WILLIAM, ed. (1966), *Philosophical Analysis and History*, New York: Harper & Row.

DRAY, WILLIAM H. (1967), 'Singular Hypotheticals and Historical Explanation,' in Gross, ed. (1967), pp. 181–203.

DURKHEIM, ÉMILE (1915), *The Elementary Forms of the Religious Life*, London: Allen & Unwin.

ERASMUS, CHARLES (1967), Review of Barringer, Blanksten and Mack, eds (1965), in *American Anthropologist*, 69, pp. 416–17.

EVANS-PRITCHARD, E. E. (1940), *The Nuer*, Oxford: Clarendon Press.

FEIGL, HERBERT and SELLARS, WILFRID, eds (1949), *Readings in Philosophical Analysis*, New York: Appleton-Century-Crofts.

FREEMAN, DEREK (1965), 'Anthropology, Psychiatry and the Doctrine of Cultural Relativism,' *Man*, 65, pp. 65–7.

FRIED, MORTON H., ed. (1959), *Readings in Anthropology, Vol. II: Cultural Anthropology*, New York: Crowell.

GARDINER, PATRICK (1952), *The Nature of Historical Explanation*, London: Oxford University Press.

GEERTZ, CLIFFORD (1957), 'Ritual and Social Change: a Javanese Example,' *American Anthropologist*, 59, pp. 32–53.

GELLNER, ERNEST (1962), 'Concepts and Society,' *Transactions of the Fifth World Congress of Sociology*, 1, pp. 153–83.

GELLNER, ERNEST (1968), 'The New Idealism,' in Lakatos and Musgrave, eds (1968), pp. 370–406.

GILL, JERRY H., ed. (1969), *Philosophy Today, No. 2*. London: Macmillan.

GINSBERG, MORRIS (1953), 'On the Diversity of Morals,' *Journal of the Royal Anthropological Institute*, 83, pp. 117–35.

GOLDMAN, IRVING (1955), 'Status Rivalry and Cultural Evolution in Polynesia,' *American Anthropologist*, 57, pp. 680–97.

GOLDMAN, IRVING (1958), 'Variations in Polynesian Social Organization,' *Journal of the Polynesian Society*, 66, pp. 374–90.

GOLDMAN, IRVING (1960), 'The Evolution of Polynesian Societies,' in Diamond, ed. (1960), pp. 687–712.

GOLDMAN, IRVING (1970), *Ancient Polynesian Society*, University of Chicago Press.

GOODENOUGH, WARD H. (1971), 'Culture, Language and Society,' *McCaleb Module in Anthropology*, Addison-Wesley Publishing Co.

GOODY, JACK, ed. (1958), *The Developmental Cycle in Domestic Groups*, Cambridge University Press.

GROSS, LLEWELLYN, ed. (1967), *Sociological Theory: Inquiries and Paradigms*, New York: Harper & Row.

GRUNER, ROLF (1967), 'Understanding in the Social Sciences and History,' *Inquiry*, 10, pp. 151–63.

HAMMEL, E. A., ed. (1965), 'Formal Semantic Analysis,' *American Anthropologist*, 67, No. 5, Pt. 2.

HANSON, F. ALLAN (1970a), *Rapan Lifeways: Society and History on a Polynesian Island*, Boston: Little, Brown.

HANSON, F. ALLAN (1970b), 'The Rapan Theory of Conception,' *American Anthropologist*, 72, pp. 1444–7.

HANSON, F. ALLAN (1970c), 'Understanding in Philosophical Anthropology,' *Journal of the Anthropological Society of Oxford*, 1, pp. 61–70.

HANSON, F. ALLAN (1973), 'Political Change in Tahiti and Samoa: an Exercise in Experimental Anthropology,' *Ethnology*, 12, pp. 1–13.

HANSON, F. ALLAN and MARTIN, REX (1973), 'The Problem of Other Cultures,' *Philosophy of the Social Sciences*, 3, pp. 191–208.

HANSON, N. R. (1958), *Patterns of Discovery*, Cambridge University Press.

HARRÉ, R. (1970), *The Principles of Scientific Thinking*, University of Chicago Press.

HARRÉ, R. and SECORD, P. F. (1972), *The Explanation of Social Behaviour*, Oxford: Blackwell.

HARRIS, MARVIN (1964), *The Nature of Cultural Things*, New York: Random House.

HART, C. W. M. and PILLING, A. R. (1960), *The Tiwi of North Australia*, New York: Holt, Rinehart & Winston.

HEMPEL, CARL G. (1965), *Aspects of Scientific Explanation and Other Essays*, New York: Free Press.

HEMPEL, CARL G. (1966a), *Philosophy of Natural Science*, Englewood Cliffs, N.J.: Prentice-Hall.

HEMPEL, CARL G. (1966b), 'Explanation in Science and in History,' in Dray, ed. (1966), pp. 95–126.

HERSKOVITS, M. H. (1948), *Man and His Works*, New York: Knopf.

HESSE, MARY (1966), *Models and Analogies in Science*, University of Notre Dame Press.

HICKS, JOHN, ed. (1964), *Faith and the Philosophers*, London: Macmillan.

HODGES, H. A. (1944), *Wilhelm Dilthey: An Introduction*, London: Routledge & Kegan Paul.

HOLLIS, MARTIN (1968), 'Reason and Ritual,' *Philosophy*, 43, pp. 231–47.

HOMANS, G. C. (1964), 'Bringing Men Back In,' *American Sociological Review*, 29, pp. 809–18.

HOMANS, G. C. (1967), *The Nature of Social Science*, New York: Harcourt, Brace & World.

HOMANS, G. C. and SCHNEIDER, D. M. (1955), *Marriage, Authority, and Final Causes*, Chicago: Free Press.

HOWARD, ALAN (1963), 'Land, Activity Systems, and Decision-Making Models in Rotuma,' *Ethnology*, 2, pp. 407–40.

HOWARD, ALAN (1969), 'Recent Trends in Polynesian Social Anthropology,' *Anthropologica* (n.s.), 11, pp. 19–30.

JARVIE, I. C. (1964), *The Revolution in Anthropology*, London: Routledge & Kegan Paul.

JARVIE, I. C. (1968), 'The Emergence of Social Anthropology from Philosophy,' *Philosophical Forum* (n.s.), 1, pp. 73–84.

JARVIE, I. C. (1970), 'Understanding and Explanation in Sociology and Social Anthropology,' in Borger and Cioffi, eds (1970), pp. 231–48.

JARVIE, I. C. (1972), *Concepts and Society*, London: Routledge & Kegan Paul.

JARVIE, I. C. and AGASSI, J. (1967), 'The Problem of the Rationality of Magic,' *British Journal of Sociology*, 18, pp. 55–74.

JONES, J. A. (1971) 'Operant Psychology and the Study of Culture,' *Current Anthropology*, 12, pp. 171–89.

KANT, IMMANUEL (1912), *Kant's Prolegomena to Any Future Metaphysics*, Paul Carus, ed., Chicago: Open Court.

KAPLAN, DAVID (1965), 'The Superorganic: Science or Metaphysics?,' *American Anthropologist*, 67, pp. 958–74.

KAPLAN, DAVID and MANNERS, ROBERT A. (1972), *Culture Theory*, Englewood Cliffs, N.J.: Prentice-Hall.

KROEBER, A. L. (1917), 'The Superorganic,' *American Anthropologist*, 19, pp. 163–213.

KROEBER, A. L. (1919), 'On the Principle of Order in Civilization as Exemplified by Changes of Fashion,' *American Anthropologist*, 21, pp. 235–63.

KROEBER, A. L. (1952), *The Nature of Culture*, University of Chicago Press.

KUHN, THOMAS (1962), *The Structure of Scientific Revolutions*, University of Chicago Press.

LADD, JOHN, ed. (1973), *Ethical Relativism*, Belmont, Cal.: Wadsworth.

LAKATOS, IMRE and MUSGRAVE, ALAN, eds (1968), *Problems in the Philosophy of Science. Proceedings of the International Colloquium, London, 1965*, Vol. 3, Amsterdam: North Holland Press.

LANGER, SUZANNE (1957), *Philosophy in a New Key*, 3rd ed., Cambridge, Mass.: Harvard University Press.

LEACH, E. R. (1958), 'Concerning Trobriand Clans and the Kinship Category *Tabu*,' in Goody, ed. (1958), pp. 120–45.

LEON-PORTILLA, MIGUEL (1966), 'Pre-Hispanic Thought,' in De La Cueva *et al.* (1966), pp. 2–56.

LEONI, BRUNO (1961), 'Some Reflections on the "Relativistic" Meaning of *Wertfreiheit* in the Study of Man,' in Schoeck and Wiggins, eds (1961), pp. 158–74.

LÉVI-STRAUSS, CLAUDE (1949), *Les Structures Élémentaires de la Parenté*, Paris: Presses Universitaires de France.

LEWIS, C. I. (1949), 'Experience and Meaning,' in Feigl and Sellars, eds (1949), pp. 128–45.

LOUCH, A. R. (1966), *Explanation and Human Action*, Berkeley: University of California Press.

LOUNSBURY, FLOYD (1965), 'Another View of the Trobriand Kinship Categories,' in Hammel, ed. (1965), pp. 142–85.

LUKES, STEVEN (1967), 'Some Problems about Rationality,' *Archives Européennes de Sociologie*, 8, pp. 247–64.

MACE, C. A., ed. (1966), *British Philosophy in the Mid-Century*, 2nd ed., London: Allen & Unwin.

MACINTYRE, ALASDAIR (1964), 'Is Understanding Religion Compatible with Believing?,' in Hicks, ed. (1964), pp. 115–33.

MACINTYRE, ALASDAIR (1967), 'The Idea of a Social Science,' *Aristotelian Society*, Supplementary Volume 41, pp. 94–114.

MCMANUS, REV. EDWIN, SJ (1959), 'Catholic Doctrine and Cultural Relativism,' *American Anthropologist*, 61, p. 683.

MANDELBAUM, DAVID G., LASKER, GABRIEL W., and ALBERT, ETHEL M., eds (1963), *The Teaching of Anthropology*, American Anthropological Association, Memoir 94.

MANNINEN, J. and TUOMELA, R., eds (1975), *Essays on Explanation and Understanding*, Synthese Library, Dordrecht and Boston: Reidel.

MAQUET, JACQUES J. (1964), 'Some Epistemological Remarks on the Cultural Philosophies and their Comparison,' in Northrop and Livingston, eds (1964), pp. 13–31.

MARQUIS, DONALD (1973), 'Historical Explanation: a Reconsideration of the New Popper-Hempel Theory,' *Southwestern Journal of Philosophy*, 4, pp. 101–8.

MARTIN, REX (1975), 'Explanation and Understanding in History,' in Manninen and Tuomela, eds (1975).

MIDDLETON, JOHN (1965), *The Lugbara of Uganda*, New York: Holt, Rinehart & Winston.

MILLER, WALTER B. (1955), 'Two Concepts of Authority,' *American Anthropologist*, 57, pp. 271–89.

MOODY, EDWARD J. (1971), 'Urban Witches,' in Spradley and McCurdy, eds (1971), pp. 280–90.

MURDOCK, G. P. (1965), *Culture and Society*, University of Pittsburgh Press.

MURDOCK, G. P. (1971), 'Anthropology's Mythology,' *Royal Anthropological Institute Proceedings*, pp. 17–24.

NADEL, S. F. (1954), *Nupe Religion*, London: Routledge & Kegan Paul.

NAGEL, ERNEST (1934), 'Verifiability, Truth and Verification,' *Journal of Philosophy*, 31, pp. 141–8.

NAGEL, ERNEST (1966), 'Letter to the Editor,' *Scientific American*, 214(4), pp. 8–9, April.

NEEDHAM, RODNEY (1962), *Structure and Sentiment*, University of Chicago Press.

NEEDHAM, RODNEY (1972), *Belief, Language, and Experience*, University of Chicago Press.

NIELSEN, KAI (1966), 'Ethical Relativism and the Facts of Cultural Relativity,' *Social Research*, 33, pp. 531–51.

NIELSEN, KAI (1971), 'Anthropology and Ethics,' *Journal of Value Inquiry*, 5, pp. 253–66.

NORTHROP, F. S. C. and LIVINGSTON, HELEN H., eds (1964), *Cross-Cultural Understanding: Epistemology in Anthropology*, New York: Harper & Row.

OBEYESEKERE, G. (1966), 'Methodological and Philosophical Relativism,' *Man* (n.s.), 1, pp. 368–74.

OGDEN, C. K. and RICHARDS, I. A. (1923), *The Meaning of Meaning*, New York: Harcourt, Brace.

OPLER, MORRIS E. (1968), 'Cultural Relativity, Modern Research, and Melville Herskovits,' *American Anthropologist*, 70, pp. 563–4.

PARSONS, TALCOTT (1937), *The Structure of Social Action*, Chicago: Free Press.

PARSONS, TALCOTT (1965), 'Evaluation and Objectivity in Social Science: an Interpretation of Max Weber's Contribution,' *International Social Science Journal*, 17, pp. 46–63.

PARSONS, TALCOTT and SHILS, EDWARD A., eds (1951), *Toward a General Theory of Action*, Cambridge, Mass.: Harvard University Press.

PASCAL, BLAISE (1925), *Œuvres de Blaise Pascal*, vol. 13, Leon Brunschvicg, ed., Paris: Librairie Hachette.

PEEL, J. D. Y. (1969), 'Understanding Alien Belief-Systems,' *British Journal of Sociology*, 20, pp. 69–84.

POPPER, K. R. (1963), *The Open Society and its Enemies*, vol. 2, Princeton University Press.

POPPER, K. R. (1968), 'On the Theory of the Objective Mind,' *Proceedings of the 14th International Congress of Philosophy, Vienna*, 1, pp. 25–53.

POPPER, K. R. (1969), 'Epistemology Without a Knowing Subject,' in Gill, ed. (1969), pp. 225–77.

RAPPAPORT, ROY A. (1967), 'Ritual Regulation of Environmental Relations among a New Guinea People,' *Ethnology*, 6, pp. 17–31.

RAPPAPORT, ROY A. (1968), *Pigs for the Ancestors*, New Haven, Conn.: Yale Univeristy Press.

RAPPAPORT, ROY A. (1971), 'Nature, Culture, and Ecological Anthropology,' in Shapiro, ed. (1971), pp. 237–67.

REDFIELD, ROBERT (1953), *The Primitive World and its Transformations*, Ithaca, N.Y.: Cornell University Press.

REDFIELD, ROBERT (1973), 'The Universally Human and the Culturally Variable,' in Ladd, ed. (1973), pp. 129–43.

RICHARDS, A. I. (1967), 'African Systems of Thought: an Anglo-French Dialogue,' *Man* (n.s.), 2, pp. 286–98.

RICKMAN, H. P. (1960), 'The Reaction Against Positivism and Dilthey's Concept of Understanding,' *British Journal of Sociology*, 11, pp. 307–18.

RICKMAN, H. P. (1967), *Understanding and the Human Studies*, London: Heinemann.

RUNCIMAN, W. G. (1972), *A Critique of Max Weber's Philosophy of Social Science*, Cambridge University Press.

RYLE, GILBERT (1949), *The Concept of Mind*, London: Hutchinson.

RYLE, GILBERT (1966), 'The Theory of Meaning,' in Mace, ed. (1966), pp. 239–64.

RYNIN, DAVID (1964), 'Donagan on Collingwood: Absolute Presuppositions, Truth and Metaphysics,' *Review of Metaphysics*, 18, pp. 301–33.

SAHLINS, MARSHALL D. (1957), 'Differentiation by Adaptation in Polynesian Societies,' *Journal of the Polynesian Society*, 66, pp. 291–300.

SAHLINS, MARSHALL D. (1958), *Social Stratification in Polynesia*, Seattle: University of Washington Press.

SANDAY, PEGGY R. (1968), 'The "Psychological Reality" of American-

English Kinship Terms: an Information-Processing Approach,' *American Anthropologist*, 70, pp. 508–23.

SCHLICK, MORITZ (1949), 'Meaning and Verification,' in Feigl and Sellars, eds (1949), pp. 146–70.

SCHMIDT, P. F. (1955), 'Some Criticisms of Cultural Relativism,' *Journal of Philosophy*, 52, pp. 780–91.

SCHNEIDER, DAVID M. (1968), *American Kinship: a Cultural Account*, Englewood Cliffs, N.J.: Prentice-Hall.

SCHOECK, H. and WIGGINS, J. W., eds (1961), *Relativism and the Study of Man*, Princeton, N.J.: Van Nostrand.

SHAPIRO, HARRY L., ed. (1971), *Man, Culture and Society*, 2nd ed., London: Oxford University Press.

SILVERMAN, MARTIN (1971), *Disconcerting Issue: Meaning and Struggle in a Resettled Pacific Community*, University of Chicago Press.

SKINNER, B. F. (1953), *Science and Human Behavior*, New York: Macmillan.

SOROKIN, PITIRIM A. (1941), *Social and Cultural Dynamics, Vol. 4: Basic Problems, Principles, and Methods*, New York: American Book Co.

SPIRO, MELFORD E. (1951), 'Culture and Personality: the Natural History of a False Dichotomy,' *Psychiatry*, 14, pp. 19–46.

SPRADLEY, JAMES P., ed. (1972), *Culture and Cognition: Rules, Maps, and Plans*, San Francisco: Chandler.

SPRADLEY, JAMES P. and MCCURDY, DAVID W., eds (1971), *Conformity and Conflict: Readings in Cultural Anthropology*, Boston: Little, Brown.

STARK, W. (1958), *The Sociology of Knowledge*, London: Routledge & Kegan Paul.

STENNING, DEREK J. (1957), 'Transhumance, Migratory Drift, Migration: Patterns of Pastoral Fulani Nomadism,' *Journal of the Royal Anthropological Institute*, 87, pp. 57–73.

SUMNER, WILLIAM GRAHAM (1906), *Folkways*, Boston: Ginn.

SYLVESTER, ROBERT P. (1959), 'A Comment on Some Further Comments on Cultural Relativism,' *American Anthropologist*, 61, pp. 882–6.

TENNEKES, J. (1971), *Anthropology, Relativism and Method*. Assen: Van Gorcum.

TOULMIN, STEPHEN (1953), *The Philosophy of Science*, London: Hutchinson.

TOULMIN, STEPHEN (1966), Review of Hempel (1965), in *Scientific American*, 214(2), pp. 129–33, February.

TURNER, VICTOR W. (1967), *The Forest of Symbols*, Ithaca, N.Y.: Cornell University Press.

TURNER, VICTOR W. (1973), 'Symbols in African Ritual,' *Science*, 179, pp. 1100–5.

TUTTLE, HOWARD NELSON (1969), *Wilhelm Dilthey's Philosophy of Historical Understanding: a Critical Analysis*, Leiden: E. J. Brill.

VIVAS, ELISEO (1961), 'Reiterations and Second Thoughts on Cultural Relativism,' in Shoeck and Wiggins, eds (1961), pp. 45–73.

WAISMANN, F. (1965), *The Principles of Linguistic Philosophy*, R. Harré, ed., London: Macmillan.

WALLACE, ANTHONY F. C. (1962), 'Culture and Cognition,' *Science*, 135, pp. 351–7.

WALLACE, ANTHONY F. C. (1965), 'The Problem of the Psychological Validity of Componential Analyses,' in Hammel, ed. (1965), pp. 229–48.

WALLACE, ANTHONY F. C. (1970), *Culture and Personality*, 2nd ed., New York: Random House.

WALSH, W. H. (1967), *An Introduction to Philosophy of History*, 3rd ed., London: Hutchinson.

WATSON, PATTY JO, LE BLANC, STEVEN A., and REDMAN, CHARLES L. (1971), *Explanation in Archeology: an Explicitly Scientific Approach*, New York: Columbia University Press.

WEBER, MAX (1947), *The Theory of Social and Economic Organization*, Talcott Parsons and A. M. Henderson, trs and eds, New York: Oxford University Press.

WEBER, MAX (1949), *The Methodology of the Social Sciences*, Edward A. Shils and Henry A. Finch, trs and eds, Chicago: Free Press.

WEBER, MAX (1958), *The Protestant Ethic and the Spirit of Capitalism*, Talcott Parsons, tr., New York: Scribners.

WELLMAN, CARL (1963), 'The Ethical Implications of Cultural Relativity,' *Journal of Philosophy*, 60, pp. 169–84.

WHITE, ALAN R. (1967), *The Philosophy of Mind*, New York: Random House.

WHITE, LESLIE A. (1949), *The Science of Culture*, New York: Farrar, Straus and Giroux.

WHITE, LESLIE A. (1959), 'The Concept of Culture,' *American Anthropologist*, 61, pp. 227–51.

WHITE, LESLIE (1969), *The Science of Culture*, 2nd ed., New York: Farrar, Straus and Giroux.

WILSON, BRYAN, R., ed. (1970), *Rationality*, Evanston and New York: Harper & Row.

WILSON, MONICA (1957), *Rituals of Kinship Among the Nyakyusa*, London: Oxford University Press.

WINCH, PETER (1958), *The Idea of a Social Science*, London: Routledge & Kegan Paul.

WINCH, PETER (1964), 'Understanding a Primitive Society,' *American Philosophical Quarterly*, 1, pp. 307–24.

WISDOM, J. O. (1963), 'Metamorphoses of the Verifiability Theory of Meaning,' *Mind*, 72, pp. 335–47.

WITTFOGEL, KARL A. (1959), 'The Theory of Oriental Society,' in Fried, ed. (1959), pp. 94–113.

WITTGENSTEIN, LUDWIG (1958), *The Blue and Brown Books*, New York: Harper & Row.

WITTGENSTEIN, LUDWIG (1968), *Philosophical Investigations*, 3rd ed., G. E. M. Anscombe, tr., Oxford: Basil Blackwell.

WOLF, ERIC R. (1964), *Anthropology*, Englewood Cliffs, N.J.: Prentice-Hall.

WOOD, OSCAR P. and PITCHER, GEORGE, eds (1970), *Ryle: a Collection of Critical Essays*, Garden City, N.Y.: Doubleday.

YABLONSKY, LEWIS (1968), *The Hippie Trip*, New York: Pegasus.

Index

I am indebted to Louise Hanson for technical assistance in compiling this index.

Routledge Social Science Series

Routledge & Kegan Paul   London and Boston

68–74 Carter Lane   London EC4V 5EL
9 Park Street   Boston   Mass 02108

Contents

*Authors wishing to submit manuscripts for any series in
this catalogue should send them to the Social Science Editor,
Routledge & Kegan Paul Ltd, 68–74 Carter Lane,
London EC4V 5EL*

●*Books so marked are available in paperback*
All books are in Metric Demy 8vo format (216 × 138mm approx.)

International Library of Sociology

General Editor   John Rex

GENERAL SOCIOLOGY

Barnsley, J. H. The Social Reality of Ethics. *464 pp.*
Belshaw, Cyril. The Conditions of Social Performance. *An Exploratory Theory. 144 pp.*
Brown, Robert. Explanation in Social Science. *208 pp.*
  ● Rules and Laws in Sociology. *192 pp.*
Bruford, W. H. Chekhov and His Russia. *A Sociological Study. 244 pp.*
Cain, Maureen E. Society and the Policeman's Role. *326 pp.*
Gibson, Quentin. The Logic of Social Enquiry. *240 pp.*
Glucksmann, M. Structuralist Analysis in Contemporary Social Thought. *212 pp.*
Gurvitch, Georges. Sociology of Law. *Preface by Roscoe Pound. 264 pp.*
Hodge, H. A. Wilhelm Dilthey. *An Introduction. 184 pp.*
Homans, George C. Sentiments and Activities. *336 pp.*
Johnson, Harry M. Sociology: *a Systematic Introduction. Foreword by Robert K. Merton. 710 pp.*
Mannheim, Karl. Essays on Sociology and Social Psychology. *Edited by Paul Keckskemeti. With Editorial Note by Adolph Lowe. 344 pp.*
  Systematic Sociology: *An Introduction to the Study of Society. Edited by J. S. Erös and Professor W. A. C. Stewart. 220 pp.*
Martindale, Don. The Nature and Types of Sociological Theory. *292 pp.*
●**Maus, Heinz.** A Short History of Sociology. *234 pp.*
Mey, Harald. Field-Theory. *A Study of its Application in the Social Sciences. 352 pp.*
Myrdal, Gunnar. Value in Social Theory: *A Collection of Essays on Methodology. Edited by Paul Streeten. 332 pp.*
Ogburn, William F., and **Nimkoff, Meyer F.** A Handbook of Sociology. *Preface by Karl Mannheim. 656 pp. 46 figures. 35 tables.*
Parsons, Talcott, and **Smelser, Neil J.** Economy and Society: *A Study in the Integration of Economic and Social Theory. 362 pp.*
●**Rex, John.** Key Problems of Sociological Theory. *220 pp.*
  Discovering Sociology. *278 pp.*
  Sociology and the Demystification of the Modern World. *282 pp.*
●**Rex, John** (Ed.) Approaches to Sociology. *Contributions by Peter Abell, Frank Bechhofer, Basil Bernstein, Ronald Fletcher, David Frisby, Miriam Glucksmann, Peter Lassman, Herminio Martins, John Rex, Roland Robertson, John Westergaard and Jock Young. 302 pp.*
Rigby, A. Alternative Realities. *352 pp.*
Roche, M. Phenomenology, Language and the Social Sciences. *374 pp.*
Sahay, A. Sociological Analysis. *220 pp.*
Urry, John. Reference Groups and the Theory of Revolution. *244 pp.*
Weinberg, E. Development of Sociology in the Soviet Union. *173 pp.*

FOREIGN CLASSICS OF SOCIOLOGY

●**Durkheim, Emile.** Suicide. *A Study in Sociology*. Edited and with an Introduction by George Simpson. *404 pp.*
Professional Ethics and Civic Morals. *Translated by Cornelia Brookfield. 288 pp.*

●**Gerth, H. H.,** and **Mills, C. Wright.** From Max Weber: *Essays in Sociology. 502 pp.*

●**Tönnies, Ferdinand.** Community and Association. (*Gemeinschaft und Gesellschaft.*) *Translated and Supplemented by Charles P. Loomis. Foreword by Pitirim A. Sorokin. 334 pp.*

SOCIAL STRUCTURE

Andreski, Stanislav. Military Organization and Society. *Foreword by Professor A. R. Radcliffe-Brown. 226 pp. 1 folder.*

Coontz, Sydney H. Population Theories and the Economic Interpretation. *202 pp.*

Coser, Lewis. The Functions of Social Conflict. *204 pp.*

Dickie-Clark, H. F. Marginal Situation: *A Sociological Study of a Coloured Group. 240 pp. 11 tables.*

Glaser, Barney, and **Strauss, Anselm L.** Status Passage. *A Formal Theory. 208 pp.*

Glass, D. V. (Ed.) Social Mobility in Britain. *Contributions by J. Berent, T. Bottomore, R. C. Chambers, J. Floud, D. V. Glass, J. R. Hall, H. T. Himmelweit, R. K. Kelsall, F. M. Martin, C. A. Moser, R. Mukherjee, and W. Ziegel. 420 pp.*

Jones, Garth N. Planned Organizational Change: *An Exploratory Study Using an Empirical Approach. 268 pp.*

Kelsall, R. K. Higher Civil Servants in Britain: *From 1870 to the Present Day. 268 pp. 31 tables.*

König, René. The Community. *232 pp. Illustrated.*

●**Lawton, Denis.** Social Class, Language and Education. *192 pp.*

McLeish, John. The Theory of Social Change: *Four Views Considered. 128 pp.*

Marsh, David C. The Changing Social Structure of England and Wales, 1871-1961. *288 pp.*

Mouzelis, Nicos. Organization and Bureaucracy. *An Analysis of Modern Theories. 240 pp.*

Mulkay, M. J. Functionalism, Exchange and Theoretical Strategy. *272 pp.*

Ossowski, Stanislaw. Class Structure in the Social Consciousness. *210 pp.*

Podgórecki, Adam. Law and Society. *About 300 pp.*

SOCIOLOGY AND POLITICS

Acton, T. A. Gypsy Politics and Social Change. *316 pp.*

Hechter, Michael. Internal Colonialism. *The Celtic Fringe in British National Development, 1536–1966. About 350 pp.*

Hertz, Frederick. Nationality in History and Politics: *A Psychology and Sociology of National Sentiment and Nationalism. 432 pp.*

Kornhauser, William. The Politics of Mass Society. *272 pp. 20 tables.*

Laidler, Harry W. History of Socialism. *Social-Economic Movements: An Historical and Comparative Survey of Socialism, Communism, Co-operation, Utopianism; and other Systems of Reform and Reconstruction. 992 pp.*

Lasswell, H. D. Analysis of Political Behaviour. *324 pp.*

Mannheim, Karl. Freedom, Power and Democratic Planning. *Edited by Hans Gerth and Ernest K. Bramstedt. 424 pp.*

Mansur, Fatma. Process of Independence. *Foreword by A. H. Hanson. 208 pp.*

Martin, David A. Pacifism: *an Historical and Sociological Study. 262 pp.*

Myrdal, Gunnar. The Political Element in the Development of Economic Theory. *Translated from the German by Paul Streeten. 282 pp.*

Wootton, Graham. Workers, Unions and the State. *188 pp.*

FOREIGN AFFAIRS: THEIR SOCIAL, POLITICAL AND ECONOMIC FOUNDATIONS

Mayer, J. P. Political Thought in France from the Revolution to the Fifth Republic. *164 pp.*

CRIMINOLOGY

Ancel, Marc. Social Defence: *A Modern Approach to Criminal Problems. Foreword by Leon Radzinowicz. 240 pp.*

Cain, Maureen E. Society and the Policeman's Role. *326 pp.*

Cloward, Richard A., and **Ohlin, Lloyd E.** Delinquency and Opportunity: *A Theory of Delinquent Gangs. 248 pp.*

Downes, David M. The Delinquent Solution. *A Study in Subcultural Theory. 296 pp.*

Dunlop, A. B., and **McCabe, S.** Young Men in Detention Centres. *192 pp.*

Friedlander, Kate. The Psycho-Analytical Approach to Juvenile Delinquency: *Theory, Case Studies, Treatment. 320 pp.*

Glueck, Sheldon, and **Eleanor.** Family Environment and Delinquency. *With the statistical assistance of Rose W. Kneznek. 340 pp.*

Lopez-Rey, Manuel. Crime. *An Analytical Appraisal. 288 pp.*

Mannheim, Hermann. Comparative Criminology: *a Text Book. Two volumes. 442 pp. and 380 pp.*

Morris, Terence. The Criminal Area: *A Study in Social Ecology. Foreword by Hermann Mannheim. 232 pp. 25 tables. 4 maps.*

Rock, Paul. Making People Pay. *338 pp.*

● **Taylor, Ian, Walton, Paul,** and **Young, Jock.** The New Criminology. *For a Social Theory of Deviance. 325 pp.*

SOCIAL PSYCHOLOGY

Bagley, Christopher. The Social Psychology of the Epileptic Child. *320 pp.*

Barbu, Zevedei. Problems of Historical Psychology. *248 pp.*

Blackburn, Julian. Psychology and the Social Pattern. *184 pp.*

●**Brittan, Arthur.** Meanings and Situations. *224 pp.*

Carroll, J. Break-Out from the Crystal Palace. *200 pp.*

●**Fleming, C. M.** Adolescence: Its Social Psychology. *With an Introduction to recent findings from the fields of Anthropology, Physiology, Medicine, Psychometrics and Sociometry. 288 pp.*

● The Social Psychology of Education: *An Introduction and Guide to Its Study. 136 pp.*

Homans, George C. The Human Group. *Foreword by Bernard DeVoto. Introduction by Robert K. Merton. 526 pp.*

● Social Behaviour: *its Elementary Forms. 416 pp.*

●**Klein, Josephine.** The Study of Groups. *226 pp. 31 figures. 5 tables.*

Linton, Ralph. The Cultural Background of Personality. *132 pp.*

●**Mayo, Elton.** The Social Problems of an Industrial Civilization. *With an appendix on the Political Problem. 180 pp.*

Ottaway, A. K. C. Learning Through Group Experience. *176 pp.*

Ridder, J. C. de. The Personality of the Urban African in South Africa. *A Thematic Apperception Test Study. 196 pp. 12 plates.*

●**Rose, Arnold M.** (Ed.) Human Behaviour and Social Processes: *an Interactionist Approach. Contributions by Arnold M. Rose, Ralph H. Turner, Anselm Strauss, Everett C. Hughes, E. Franklin Frazier, Howard S. Becker, et al. 696 pp.*

Smelser, Neil J. Theory of Collective Behaviour. *448 pp.*

Stephenson, Geoffrey M. The Development of Conscience. *128 pp.*

Young, Kimball. Handbook of Social Psychology. *658 pp. 16 figures. 10 tables.*

SOCIOLOGY OF THE FAMILY

Banks, J. A. Prosperity and Parenthood: *A Study of Family Planning among The Victorian Middle Classes. 262 pp.*

Bell, Colin R. Middle Class Families: *Social and Geographical Mobility. 224 pp.*

Burton, Lindy. Vulnerable Children. *272 pp.*

Gavron, Hannah. The Captive Wife: *Conflicts of Household Mothers. 190 pp.*

George, Victor, and **Wilding, Paul.** Motherless Families. *220 pp.*

Klein, Josephine. Samples from English Cultures.

   1. Three Preliminary Studies and Aspects of Adult Life in England. *447 pp.*

   2. Child-Rearing Practices and Index. *247 pp.*

Klein, Viola. Britain's Married Women Workers. *180 pp.*

   The Feminine Character. *History of an Ideology. 244 pp.*

McWhinnie, Alexina M. Adopted Children. *How They Grow Up. 304 pp.*

● **Myrdal, Alva,** and **Klein, Viola.** Women's Two Roles: *Home and Work. 238 pp. 27 tables.*

Parsons, Talcott, and **Bales, Robert F.** Family: Socialization and Interaction Process. *In collaboration with James Olds, Morris Zelditch and Philip E. Slater. 456 pp. 50 figures and tables.*

SOCIAL SERVICES

Bastide, Roger. The Sociology of Mental Disorder. *Translated from the French by Jean McNeil. 260 pp.*

Carlebach, Julius. Caring For Children in Trouble. *266 pp.*

Forder, R. A. (Ed.) Penelope Hall's Social Services of England and Wales. *352 pp.*

George, Victor. Foster Care. *Theory and Practice. 234 pp.*
  Social Security: *Beveridge and After. 258 pp.*

George, V., and **Wilding, P.** Motherless Families. *248 pp.*

●**Goetschius, George W.** Working with Community Groups. *256 pp.*

Goetschius, George W., and **Tash, Joan.** Working with Unattached Youth. *416 pp.*

Hall, M. P., and **Howes, I. V.** The Church in Social Work. *A Study of Moral Welfare Work undertaken by the Church of England. 320 pp.*

Heywood, Jean S. Children in Care: *the Development of the Service for the Deprived Child. 264 pp.*

Hoenig, J., and **Hamilton, Marian W.** The De-Segregation of the Mentally Ill. *284 pp.*

Jones, Kathleen. Mental Health and Social Policy, 1845-1959. *264 pp.*

King, Roy D., Raynes, Norma V., and **Tizard, Jack.** Patterns of Residential Care. *356 pp.*

Leigh, John. Young People and Leisure. *256 pp.*

Morris, Mary. Voluntary Work and the Welfare State. *300 pp.*

Morris, Pauline. Put Away: *A Sociological Study of Institutions for the Mentally Retarded. 364 pp.*

Nokes, P. L. The Professional Task in Welfare Practice. *152 pp.*

Timms, Noel. Psychiatric Social Work in Great Britain (1939-1962). *280 pp.*

● Social Casework: *Principles and Practice. 256 pp.*

Young, A. F. Social Services in British Industry. *272 pp.*

Young, A. F., and **Ashton, E. T.** British Social Work in the Nineteenth Century. *288 pp.*

SOCIOLOGY OF EDUCATION

Banks, Olive. Parity and Prestige in English Secondary Education: a Study in Educational Sociology. *272 pp.*

Bentwich, Joseph. Education in Israel. *224 pp. 8 pp. plates.*

●**Blyth, W. A. L.** English Primary Education. *A Sociological Description.*
  1. Schools. *232 pp.*
  2. Background. *168 pp.*

Collier, K. G. The Social Purposes of Education: *Personal and Social Values in Education. 268 pp.*

Dale, R. R., and **Griffith, S.** Down Stream: *Failure in the Grammar School. 108 pp.*

Dore, R. P. Education in Tokugawa Japan. *356 pp. 9 pp. plates.*

Evans, K. M. Sociometry and Education. *158 pp.*

●**Ford, Julienne.** Social Class and the Comprehensive School. *192 pp.*

Foster, P. J. Education and Social Change in Ghana. *336 pp. 3 maps.*

Fraser, W. R. Education and Society in Modern France. *150 pp.*

Grace, Gerald R. Role Conflict and the Teacher. *About 200 pp.*

Hans, Nicholas. New Trends in Education in the Eighteenth Century. *278 pp. 19 tables.*

● Comparative Education: *A Study of Educational Factors and Traditions. 360 pp.*

Hargreaves, David. Interpersonal Relations and Education. *432 pp.*

● Social Relations in a Secondary School. *240 pp.*

Holmes, Brian. Problems in Education. *A Comparative Approach. 336 pp.*

King, Ronald. Values and Involvement in a Grammar School. *164 pp.*

School Organization and Pupil Involvement. *A Study of Secondary Schools.*

●**Mannheim, Karl,** and **Stewart, W. A. C.** An Introduction to the Sociology of Education. *206 pp.*

Morris, Raymond N. The Sixth Form and College Entrance. *231 pp.*

●**Musgrove, F.** Youth and the Social Order. *176 pp.*

●**Ottaway, A. K. C.** Education and Society: An Introduction to the Sociology of Education. *With an Introduction by W. O. Lester Smith. 212 pp.*

Peers, Robert. Adult Education: *A Comparative Study. 398 pp.*

Pritchard, D. G. Education and the Handicapped: *1760 to 1960. 258 pp.*

Richardson, Helen. Adolescent Girls in Approved Schools. *308 pp.*

Stratta, Erica. The Education of Borstal Boys. *A Study of their Educational Experiences prior to, and during, Borstal Training. 256 pp.*

Taylor, P. H., Reid, W. A., and **Holley, B. J.** The English Sixth Form. *A Case Study in Curriculum Research. 200 pp.*

SOCIOLOGY OF CULTURE

Eppel, E. M., and **M.** Adolescents and Morality: *A Study of some Moral Values and Dilemmas of Working Adolescents in the Context of a changing Climate of Opinion. Foreword by W. J. H. Sprott. 268 pp. 39 tables.*

●**Fromm, Erich.** The Fear of Freedom. *286 pp.*

● The Sane Society. *400 pp.*

Mannheim, Karl. Essays on the Sociology of Culture. *Edited by Ernst Mannheim in co-operation with Paul Kecskemeti. Editorial Note by Adolph Lowe. 280 pp.*

Weber, Alfred. Farewell to European History: *or The Conquest of Nihilism. Translated from the German by R. F. C. Hull. 224 pp.*

SOCIOLOGY OF RELIGION

Argyle, Michael and **Beit-Hallahmi, Benjamin.** The Social Psychology of Religion. *About 256 pp.*
Nelson, G. K. Spiritualism and Society. *313 pp.*
Stark, Werner. The Sociology of Religion. *A Study of Christendom.*
   Volume I. *Established Religion. 248 pp.*
   Volume II. *Sectarian Religion. 368 pp.*
   Volume III. *The Universal Church. 464 pp.*
   Volume IV. *Types of Religious Man. 352 pp.*
   Volume V. *Types of Religious Culture. 464 pp.*
Turner, B. S. Weber and Islam. *216 pp.*
Watt, W. Montgomery. Islam and the Integration of Society. *320 pp.*

SOCIOLOGY OF ART AND LITERATURE

Jarvie, Ian C. Towards a Sociology of the Cinema. *A Comparative Essay on the Structure and Functioning of a Major Entertainment Industry. 405 pp.*
Rust, Frances S. Dance in Society. *An Analysis of the Relationships between the Social Dance and Society in England from the Middle Ages to the Present Day. 256 pp. 8 pp. of plates.*
Schücking, L. L. The Sociology of Literary Taste. *112 pp.*
Wolff, Janet. Hermeneutic Philosophy and the Sociology of Art. *About 200 pp.*

SOCIOLOGY OF KNOWLEDGE

Diesing, P. Patterns of Discovery in the Social Sciences. *262 pp.*
● **Douglas, J. D.** (Ed.) Understanding Everyday Life. *370 pp.*
● **Hamilton, P.** Knowledge and Social Structure. *174 pp.*
Jarvie, I. C. Concepts and Society. *232 pp.*
Mannheim, Karl. Essays on the Sociology of Knowledge. *Edited by Paul Kecskemeti. Editorial Note by Adolph Lowe. 353 pp.*
Remmling, Gunter W. (Ed.) Towards the Sociology of Knowledge. *Origin and Development of a Sociological Thought Style. 463 pp.*
Stark, Werner. The Sociology of Knowledge: *An Essay in Aid of a Deeper Understanding of the History of Ideas. 384 pp.*

URBAN SOCIOLOGY

Ashworth, William. The Genesis of Modern British Town Planning: *A Study in Economic and Social History of the Nineteenth and Twentieth Centuries. 288 pp.*
Cullingworth, J. B. Housing Needs and Planning Policy: *A Restatement of the Problems of Housing Need and 'Overspill' in England and Wales. 232 pp. 44 tables. 8 maps.*

Dickinson, Robert E. City and Region: *A Geographical Interpretation* *608 pp. 125 figures.*
The West European City: *A Geographical Interpretation. 600 pp. 129 maps. 29 plates.*
● The City Region in Western Europe. *320 pp. Maps.*
Humphreys, Alexander J. New Dubliners: *Urbanization and the Irish Family. Foreword by George C. Homans. 304 pp.*
Jackson, Brian. Working Class Community: *Some General Notions raised by a Series of Studies in Northern England. 192 pp.*
Jennings, Hilda. Societies in the Making: *a Study of Development and Redevelopment within a County Borough. Foreword by D. A. Clark. 286 pp.*
●**Mann, P. H.** An Approach to Urban Sociology. *240 pp.*
Morris, R. N., and **Mogey, J.** The Sociology of Housing. *Studies at Berinsfield. 232 pp. 4 pp. plates.*
Rosser, C., and **Harris, C.** The Family and Social Change. *A Study of Family and Kinship in a South Wales Town. 352 pp. 8 maps.*

RURAL SOCIOLOGY

Chambers, R. J. H. Settlement Schemes in Tropical Africa: *A Selective Study. 268 pp.*
Haswell, M. R. The Economics of Development in Village India. *120 pp.*
Littlejohn, James. Westrigg: *the Sociology of a Cheviot Parish. 172 pp. 5 figures.*
Mayer, Adrian C. Peasants in the Pacific. *A Study of Fiji Indian Rural Society. 248 pp. 20 plates.*
Williams, W. M. The Sociology of an English Village: *Gosforth. 272 pp. 12 figures. 13 tables.*

SOCIOLOGY OF INDUSTRY AND DISTRIBUTION

Anderson, Nels. Work and Leisure. *280 pp.*
●**Blau, Peter M.,** and **Scott, W. Richard.** Formal Organizations: *a Comparative approach. Introduction and Additional Bibliography by J. H. Smith. 326 pp.*
Eldridge, J. E. T. Industrial Disputes. *Essays in the Sociology of Industrial Relations. 288 pp.*
Hetzler, Stanley. Applied Measures for Promoting Technological Growth. *352 pp.*
Technological Growth and Social Change. *Achieving Modernization. 269 pp.*
Hollowell, Peter G. The Lorry Driver. *272 pp.*
Jefferys, Margot, *with the assistance of Winifred Moss.* Mobility in the Labour Market: *Employment Changes in Battersea and Dagenham. Preface by Barbara Wootton. 186 pp. 51 tables.*

Millerson, Geoffrey. The Qualifying Associations: *a Study in Professionalization. 320 pp.*

Smelser, Neil J. Social Change in the Industrial Revolution: *An Application of Theory to the Lancashire Cotton Industry, 1770-1840. 468 pp. 12 figures. 14 tables.*

Williams, Gertrude. Recruitment to Skilled Trades. *240 pp.*

Young, A. F. Industrial Injuries Insurance: *an Examination of British Policy. 192 pp.*

DOCUMENTARY

Schlesinger, Rudolf (Ed.) Changing Attitudes in Soviet Russia.
   2. The Nationalities Problem and Soviet Administration. *Selected Readings on the Development of Soviet Nationalities Policies. Introduced by the editor. Translated by W. W. Gottlieb. 324 pp.*

ANTHROPOLOGY

Ammar, Hamed. Growing up in an Egyptian Village: *Silwa, Province of Aswan. 336 pp.*

Brandel-Syrier, Mia. Reeftown Elite. *A Study of Social Mobility in a Modern African Community on the Reef. 376 pp.*

Crook, David, and **Isabel.** Revolution in a Chinese Village: *Ten Mile Inn. 230 pp. 8 plates. 1 map.*

Dickie-Clark, H. F. The Marginal Situation. *A Sociological Study of a Coloured Group. 236 pp.*

Dube, S. C. Indian Village. *Foreword by Morris Edward Opler. 276 pp. 4 plates.*
   India's Changing Villages: *Human Factors in Community Development. 260 pp. 8 plates. 1 map.*

Firth, Raymond. Malay Fishermen. *Their Peasant Economy. 420 pp. 17 pp. plates.*

Firth, R., Hubert, J., and **Forge, A.** Families and their Relatives. *Kinship in a Middle-Class Sector of London: An Anthropological Study. 456 pp.*

Gulliver, P. H. Social Control in an African Society: a Study of the Arusha, Agricultural Masai of Northern Tanganyika. *320 pp. 8 plates. 10 figures.*
   Family Herds. *288 pp.*

Ishwaran, K. Shivapur. *A South Indian Village. 216 pp.*
   Tradition and Economy in Village India: *An Interactionist Approach. Foreword by Conrad Arensburg. 176 pp.*

Jarvie, Ian C. The Revolution in Anthropology. *268 pp.*

Jarvie, Ian C., and **Agassi, Joseph.** Hong Kong. *A Society in Transition. 396 pp. Illustrated with plates and maps.*

Little, Kenneth L. Mende of Sierra Leone. *308 pp. and folder.*
   Negroes in Britain. *With a New Introduction and Contemporary Study by Leonard Bloom. 320 pp.*

Lowie, Robert H. Social Organization. *494 pp.*
Mayer, Adrian C. Caste and Kinship in Central India: *A Village and its Region. 328 pp. 16 plates. 15 figures. 16 tables.*
Peasants in the Pacific. *A Study of Fiji Indian Rural Society. 248 pp.*
Smith, Raymond T. The Negro Family in British Guiana: *Family Structure and Social Status in the Villages. With a Foreword by Meyer Fortes. 314 pp. 8 plates. 1 figure. 4 maps.*

SOCIOLOGY AND PHILOSOPHY

Barnsley, John H. The Social Reality of Ethics. *A Comparative Analysis of Moral Codes. 448 pp.*
Diesing, Paul. Patterns of Discovery in the Social Sciences. *362 pp.*
●**Douglas, Jack D.** (Ed.) Understanding Everyday Life. *Toward the Reconstruction of Sociological Knowledge. Contributions by Alan F. Blum. Aaron W. Cicourel, Norman K. Denzin, Jack D. Douglas, John Heeren, Peter McHugh, Peter K. Manning, Melvin Power, Matthew Speier, Roy Turner, D. Lawrence Wieder, Thomas P. Wilson and Don H. Zimmerman. 370 pp.*
Jarvie, Ian C. Concepts and Society. *216 pp.*
Pelz, Werner. The Scope of Understanding in Sociology. *Towards a more radical reorientation in the social humanistic sciences. 283 pp.*
Roche, Maurice. Phenomenology, Language and the Social Sciences. *371 pp.*
Sahay, Arun. Sociological Analysis. *212 pp.*
Sklair, Leslie. The Sociology of Progress. *320 pp.*

International Library of Anthropology
General Editor Adam Kuper

Brown, Paula. The Chimbu. *A Study of Change in the New Guinea Highlands. 151 pp.*
Lloyd, P. C. Power and Independence. *Urban Africans' Perception of Social Inequality. 264 pp.*
Pettigrew, Joyce. Robber Noblemen. *A Study of the Political System of the Sikh Jats. 284 pp.*
Van Den Berghe, Pierre L. Power and Privilege at an African University. *278 pp.*

International Library of Social Policy
General Editor Kathleen Jones

Bayley, M. Mental Handicap and Community Care. *426 pp.*
Butler, J. R. Family Doctors and Public Policy. *208 pp.*
Holman, Robert. Trading in Children. *A Study of Private Fostering. 355 pp.*

Jones, Kathleen. History of the Mental Health Service. *428 pp.*

Thomas, J. E. The English Prison Officer since 1850: *A Study in Conflict. 258 pp.*

Woodward, J. To Do the Sick No Harm. *A Study of the British Voluntary Hospital System to 1875. About 220 pp.*

International Library of Welfare and Philosophy

General Editors Noel Timms and David Watson

● **Plant, Raymond.** Community and Ideology. *104 pp.*

Primary Socialization, Language and Education

General Editor Basil Bernstein

Bernstein, Basil. Class, Codes and Control. *2 volumes.*
   1. *Theoretical Studies Towards a Sociology of Language. 254 pp.*
   2. *Applied Studies Towards a Sociology of Language. About 400 pp.*
Brandis, W., and **Bernstein, B.** Selection and Control. *176 pp.*
Brandis, Walter, and **Henderson, Dorothy.** Social Class, Language and Communication. *288 pp.*
Cook-Gumperz, Jenny. Social Control and Socialization. *A Study of Class Differences in the Language of Maternal Control. 290 pp.*
● **Gahagan, D. M.,** and **G. A.** Talk Reform. *Exploration in Language for Infant School Children. 160 pp.*
Robinson, W. P., and **Rackstraw, Susan D. A.** A Question of Answers. *2 volumes. 192 pp. and 180 pp.*
Turner, Geoffrey J., and **Mohan, Bernard A.** A Linguistic Description and Computer Programme for Children's Speech. *208 pp.*

Reports of the Institute of Community Studies

Cartwright, Ann. Human Relations and Hospital Care. *272 pp.*
●   Parents and Family Planning Services. *306 pp.*
   Patients and their Doctors. *A Study of General Practice. 304 pp.*
● **Jackson, Brian.** Streaming: *an Education System in Miniature. 168 pp.*
Jackson, Brian, and **Marsden, Dennis.** Education and the Working Class: *Some General Themes raised by a Study of 88 Working-class Children in a Northern Industrial City. 268 pp. 2 folders.*
Marris, Peter. The Experience of Higher Education. *232 pp. 27 tables.*
   Loss and Change. *192 pp.*

Marris, Peter, and Rein, Martin. Dilemmas of Social Reform. *Poverty and Community Action in the United States. 256 pp.*

Marris, Peter, and Somerset, Anthony. African Businessmen. *A Study of Entrepreneurship and Development in Kenya. 256 pp.*

Mills, Richard. Young Outsiders: *a Study in Alternative Communities. 216 pp.*

Runciman, W. G. Relative Deprivation and Social Justice. *A Study of Attitudes to Social Inequality in Twentieth-Century England. 352 pp.*

Willmott, Peter. Adolescent Boys in East London. *230 pp.*

Willmott, Peter, and Young, Michael. Family and Class in a London Suburb. *202 pp. 47 tables.*

Young, Michael. Innovation and Research in Education. *192 pp.*

●Young, Michael, and McGeeney, Patrick. Learning Begins at Home. *A Study of a Junior School and its Parents. 128 pp.*

Young, Michael, and Willmott, Peter. Family and Kinship in East London. *Foreword by Richard M. Titmuss. 252 pp. 39 tables.*
The Symmetrical Family. *410 pp.*

Reports of the Institute for Social Studies in Medical Care

Cartwright, Ann, Hockey, Lisbeth, and Anderson, John L. Life Before Death. *310 pp.*

Dunnell, Karen, and Cartwright, Ann. Medicine Takers, Prescribers and Hoarders. *190 pp.*

Medicine, Illness and Society

General Editor W. M. Williams

Robinson, David. The Process of Becoming Ill. *142 pp.*

Stacey, Margaret, *et al.* Hospitals, Children and Their Families. *The Report of a Pilot Study. 202 pp.*

Monographs in Social Theory

General Editor Arthur Brittan

●Barnes, B. Scientific Knowledge and Sociological Theory. *About 200 pp.*

Bauman, Zygmunt. Culture as Praxis. *204 pp.*

● Dixon, Keith. Sociological Theory. *Pretence and Possibility. 142 pp.*

●Smith, Anthony D. The Concept of Social Change. *A Critique of the Functionalist Theory of Social Change. 208 pp.*

Routledge Social Science Journals

The British Journal of Sociology. *Edited by Terence P. Morris. Vol. 1, No. 1, March 1950 and Quarterly. Roy. 8vo. Back numbers available. An international journal with articles on all aspects of sociology.*

Economy and Society. *Vol. 1, No. 1. February 1972 and Quarterly. Metric Roy. 8vo. A journal for all social scientists covering sociology, philosophy, anthropology, economics and history. Back numbers available.*

Year Book of Social Policy in Britain, The. *Edited by Kathleen Jones. 1971. Published annually.*

Printed in Great Britain by Unwin Brothers Limited
The Gresham Press Old Woking Surrey
A member of the Staples Printing Group